Get Promoted

With a track record of 19 years' career experience across leadership advisory services, including strategy consulting, head-hunting and executive coaching, Niamh O'Keeffe has become an internationally regarded expert on the performance acceleration of leaders and their teams. Niamh spent the first eight years of her career with Accenture as a strategy and management consultant, followed by two years as Chief Executive of a non-profit education and training centre and finally a headhunter in the City of London working mostly with Barclays. In 2004, Niamh established First100, a leadership and performance acceleration consultancy. Niamh is the author of six books. The most recent is *Future Shaper: How Leaders Can Take Charge in an Uncertain World*.

Niamh O'Keeffe

Get Promoted

BUSINESS

PENGUIN BUSINESS

UK | USA | Canada | Ireland | Australia
India | New Zealand | South Africa

Penguin Business is part of the Penguin Random
House group of companies whose addresses can
be found at global.penguinrandomhouse.com

Penguin
Random House
UK

First published 2020
001

Copyright © Niamh O'Keeffe, 2020

The moral right of the author has been asserted

Text design by Richard Marston
Set in 11.75/14.75 pt Minion Pro
Typeset by Jouve (UK), Milton Keynes
Printed and bound in Great Britain by
Clays Ltd, Elcograf S.p.A.

A CIP catalogue record for this book is available
from the British Library

ISBN: 978-0-241-46527-1

Follow us on LinkedIn: https://www.linkedin.com/
company/penguin-connect

www.greenpenguin.co.uk

MIX
Paper from
responsible sources
FSC
www.fsc.org   FSC® C018179

Penguin Random House is committed to a
sustainable future for our business, our readers
and our planet. This book is made from Forest
Stewardship Council® certified paper.

Thank you to Celia and Martina from Penguin, to Eimee and to my family.

I wrote this book during the 2020 COVID-19 London lockdown. It gave me focus, and I hope it inspires focus in my readers as they progress their careers in an increasingly uncertain world. With that in mind, I would like to dedicate this book to my nieces and nephews, and – of course – to my daughter Meera, whose bright smile and beautiful spirit inspire me every day.

Contents

Introduction

If you follow the advice in this book, you will get promoted.

Having worked as a leadership advisor with many clients, over many years, I am in a position to be able to spot patterns of behaviour. As a consultant to an organization, not a member of the organization, I operate outside the system. This gives me a unique perspective on how the system works.

My observations have led me to realize that promotions don't always happen in the way that people assume. Getting promoted is not just about working hard and doing a good job. If securing your next promotion was as simple as that, then surely you wouldn't have needed to pick up this book in the first place!

If you have started to realize that promotion decisions are more nuanced, read on. If you feel like you are blocked in some way – within yourself, or by others – and you don't know why, read on. If you have been blindsided by peers getting promoted, and are concerned you are being left behind, then read on. If you feel you lack the 'secret code' to unlock what it really takes to get ahead and are starting to feel resentful or frustrated, then read on.

In this book I will provide you with insights about how promotions really work, and what you need to do to secure your next role. I will decode the mysteries and help you to get promoted – but even better than that, I will help you to be strategic about your career and figure out how your next role fits into a longer-term strategy. That way, you will be as focused as an arrow – homing in on your target, totally clear about what you want to achieve and why – and your motivation, time and energy will be aligned accordingly.

This book is about providing you with a breakthrough approach to your next promotion, and the one after that, and the ones after that. It is about building your skills and intelligence in what it takes to get promoted.

I am on your side – and whatever your starting point, I will help you to get promoted. It is what I do for my clients, again and again, typically guiding them from 'stuck in the middle' middle management to eventual C-suite. I don't preselect my clients based on any particular criteria, specific potential or innate talent for getting to the next level. I don't conduct feedback-gathering prior to starting our work, to help assess whether the odds are stacked in their favour. I simply work with anyone who wants to get promoted, whatever their level, to help them achieve their goal – as long as they commit, and are willing to act on my advice.

At the start of my foray into coaching people on how to get promoted, the results always came faster than my clients or I expected. I noticed something interesting happening: that the momentum we created caused further momentum and acceleration, and 'suddenly' the promotion goal was realized. Now I know for sure we can always expect fast results.

I have worked for years on what it takes to get promoted. I am pleased to now be able to codify my approach in this book. Just as I help each of my clients get promoted again and again – faster and faster each time – if you are motivated to follow my advice, then it will happen even sooner than you think.

If you picked up this book, then you are either already ambitious or some part of you knows that you simply can't afford to stand still in your career and not get promoted. You likely already know that there comes a point at your company and in your career where you are either moving up or moving out. If you have been in your role for at least three years, it should be time to secure your next promotion. If you get passed over for promotion and find yourself in your current role for five years or more, then you should not take it for granted that you can keep your job for much longer. It depends on your company culture, of course, but typically there is always upward pressure from newer, younger people who are climbing the ranks and securing better positions. I don't like to use fear as motivation, but I want to be candid so that you are realistic. If you are not being driven by ambition, then you may have to be driven by practicality in order to self-improve and seek your next role. Your efforts will not go to waste. It is always good to show drive rather than be seen to be coasting in your role – especially if you are part of a competitive corporate culture where it is all about survival of the fittest.

In an attempt to go all out to help you secure your next promotion, I will leave no stone unturned in terms of tactics. I delve into all the key strategies that will take you from your current role to your dream role. If at first you find all the advice a little overwhelming, please know that you can start your promotion journey by applying just some of the ideas – over time you will be ready to add new layers of these strategies. Think of getting promoted as a skill to be mastered, not just a one-off transaction.

Look at this book as your coach, companion and guide on your get-promoted journey. For some of you, it really will be as simple as reading it once and finding an insight that immediately unlocks the door onto how to get promoted. For others, it may be worth rereading the book, and introducing new habits and behaviours gradually. Whichever way you learn, the answers are within this book – how and when to apply them is up to you.

I don't regard my advice as 'hacks' – these are genuine insights into what it takes to secure your next role and progress in your career. You will find it very empowering and self-motivating to have a clear and insightful game plan. You will feel more in control. And as you change, the people around you will notice you, and your forward momentum will propel your promotion success.

I wish you well on your journey of reading this book, applying the strategies within, and enjoying all the exciting benefits and experiences that follow.

You can connect and share your experiences, questions and stories with me at https://www.linkedin.com/in/niamhokeeffeadvisor/

1 Why you have not been promoted – yet!

You may be feeling like you have no power over your promotion, and that you are at the mercy of your superiors. In fact, you hold most – if not all – of the cards in terms of shaping your future. There are many proactive strategies you can utilize to re-platform your skills and credibility, get noticed and get promoted. But let's kick-start your journey by dispelling some of the typical misconceptions about the promotions process.

Common myths and mistakes

We would like to believe that all promotions are fair and that our company is truly the transparent meritocracy that it claims to be in the brochure. However, in reality, organizations operate in a highly social way. While everyone may aspire to a world of fairness, very often interpersonal conflicts, personal histories and preferences, pre-existing relationships and political agendas all get in the way of fact-based meritocratic decision-making.

You need to know that promotions are not always about fairness or transparency or just working hard. A lot of decisions are situational, contextualized and flawed, and they are often about timing.

The myth of meritocracy

When Shay urgently needed to fill a spot on his team, he decided not to take four months to go through the internal process of advertising, then interviewing and recruiting the best candidate within the company – because a faster workaround was to bring Sophie in from his previous company. Of course, he hadn't realized that Sophie would insist on a level upgrade to incentivize her to leave her old company, and now he is in so deep – after having persuaded his boss and HR that an external hire is necessary – that he gives Sophie what she wants and agrees the start date. All of Shay's direct reports are annoyed that an external person has been brought in, and they know she was probably paid more than an internal candidate would have been. Fair? No. Fast? Yes. Regrets? Maybe, because Shay didn't expect the backlash from his team, but it is all done now.

You probably already know that life and promotions are not fair, because you have had this experience in one form or another. Don't despair, though. Once your eyes are opened to how decisions are really made, then you can figure out how to position yourself for success.

Myth #1: Work hard and you will get promoted

You might be working extremely hard in your current role – convinced that if you just put in the extra hours, your manager will notice and reward you with that promotion you have been asking for. But this is often a false hope. It could even be one that your boss is exploiting. The promise of a promotion is often just a motivational decoy, because in reality a promotion is not always a reward for hard work. Rather, it is a bet on your future potential. Your boss, and their bosses, need to be convinced about your future potential, not just your past years of competent service. Seeing the role of promotions from this company perspective will help you understand not just the importance of demonstrating capability in your current role, but also why you need to position your current work as an example of what you could do in the future if given the responsibility.

If you are passed over for promotion, are you going to continue with the same naive, head-down, 'I will simply work harder, and get the promotion next time' response, or will you adapt your strategy? Work ethic and performance are only part of the solution.

Myth #2: The best people always get promoted

Unfortunately, it is not always the best people who get promoted. Do you think all your managers and top leaders are great role models and have the best skills for the job? Hopefully most – or at least some – do. However, organizations are not always meritocratic. People and politics have a major influence on outcomes. It is often who you know, not what you know, when it comes to getting ahead in your career. There is logic to this – if the hiring manager doesn't know you but does know your peer's name and reputation, or has a pre-existing working relationship with them, then your peer has an immediate advantage over you. Perhaps your peer has ingratiated themselves better than you with the people who make the promotion decision. You don't need to deploy the same tactics as them, but you do need to get in the game and let decision-makers know who you are and what you can offer – if you want a more level playing field.

Myth #3: The promotion process is always totally transparent

Your HR department might seek to conduct a fair and transparent promotions process, but in reality there will always be a combination of macro reasons (such as fear of an economic recession) and micro reasons (such as organizational politics) playing a determining role. Promotion decisions may be based on whose turn it is next, who was turned down last time, who fights hardest, or even whether or not they are the nephew of the CEO. Perhaps – behind closed doors – your boss is not totally committed to securing your promotion. Or they may not even be the primary decision-maker in the process. They might want to promote you but are constrained by budgets, or by their boss, and do not want to admit to you that it is not within their power to actually promote you. Perhaps you have performed well as an individual, but the team you are in has not met its targets and therefore none of you can be promoted. Maybe your boss rates you but doesn't want to lose you from the team, so holds you back from the promotion this time. There are so many covert reasons why you may not have been promoted, and these may never be shared with you. The process is not always totally transparent.

TOP TIP

Talk to people who were promoted recently within your company

Ask them how the promotion process really worked – who helped them, who was in charge, and what it was that they think swayed the decision. Because they made it through, they will likely feel very benevolent about handing down advice on how they did it. Listen to their observations and thoughts on what it took, and try to work out who and what really mattered in the promotion process.

Your willingness to challenge your own assumptions – and those of others – about how promotions really work, will help you to be more clear-sighted about how the decisions are made in your company. Open your eyes to the possibility that things are not as they first seem. We like to think that there are strict processes for promotion – and transparent ways of working. But organizations are made up of flawed people just like you and me, and are highly interpersonal places. And this dynamic is often the major determining factor at promotion time.

It is worth checking who really makes the decision about your promotion, and how such decisions are made. The best people to ask about this are those who got promoted last time (find out how they did it) and those who didn't (ask them what they think happened). Once you have a better understanding of how promotions really work in your organization, draw your own conclusions about what is rewarded in your company. Be prepared to explore what is going on in your organization and company culture – above and below the surface – so that you can figure out who and what truly matters in terms of promotion decision-making. If you can identify the real decision-makers and decode their behaviour patterns, then you can better spot the opportunities to progress faster in your organization.

Be proactive, not passive-aggressive

You have the power to create the future you want. This message of self-empowerment is the most important lesson to learn on your promotion journey. Understanding that you – not your boss, or anyone else – have the most agency to take charge of your career is the key to not just your next promotion, but to the ones after that and to your ongoing success. If you want to get promoted, you must cultivate a proactive attitude and take ownership of your strategy – what you are doing and what you are not doing – to progress.

When it comes to promotions, too many people assume that their turn will come. This overly passive strategy results in a huge number of people waiting far too long – and sometimes forever – to be noticed. When they are passed over for promotion, some people's frustration takes the form of sulking, and they withdraw temporarily from making a proper contribution or even withdraw fully by handing in their resignation. Some stay unhappy and resentful and never quite get over it. Others pursue a low-level but persistent long-term campaign of complaining to their boss. This can lead to a very negative spiral, both for them and for their relationship with their boss, which won't serve them well for promotion consideration next time either.

It is also common to use the threat of leaving to try to force the boss's hand, i.e. 'If my boss doesn't promote me, I'll leave.' This is the ultimate passive-aggressive strategy for anyone who is frustrated by their lack of progress. My advice is: don't ever threaten to leave if you don't really mean it. It may backfire if your bluff is called. Even if the threat results in a promotion in the short term, it could seriously work against you in the longer term, because this kind of behaviour comes across as self-centred and disloyal.

Leaving a good company should be your last-resort action, not the first. Of course, if you are truly unhappy, then leaving may unfortunately become necessary. If there is low chance that your boss or the promotion decision-maker will ever appreciate your potential, then leave, but test out those odds first. Start afresh with a positive and proactive approach, develop your get-promoted strategy – deploying all the skills and tools you will learn in this book – and give yourself a timeline. You have more to lose than gain by simply moving on without learning the get-promoted game.

Be very careful not to make any rash decisions about resigning and leaving your current role and company, where you have built up a good reputation over time. My general advice is never leave a role until you have another one. It's too risky – especially if the job market is not buoyant or suddenly becomes subject to unexpected macro forces like an economic downturn. The longer you are without a job, the harder it often is to get a new one. This is because prospective employers start to degrade your worth over time, wondering why you don't have a job yet and why you haven't been snapped up, and it may become a more desperate situation as you have to try even harder to convince them of your value.

In any case, resigning and moving to a new company is not always the right answer. Quite often, it is the illusion of thinking the grass is greener elsewhere. You should certainly think about moving if you can trade up for a better role, brand or culture, or a better work–life balance or platform for future opportunities. But be warned that if moving company every two to three years is your sole get-promoted strategy, it eventually becomes transparent on your CV and future bosses may not hire you. If your one trick for getting promoted is to change companies, it doesn't make for a sustainable approach. You may be regarded by potential hiring managers as not loyal – and not a good return on their hiring investment – if they think you plan on only staying a few years with them too.

Constant moving around also means you will likely have to go from premium company brands to less premium brands in order to get promoted to the next level up. If you keep trading down in order to secure your promotion, you may end up with a better job title in the short term but poorer long-term prospects – and the only way to trade back up again is to take a lesser role at a more premium brand!

Of course, there are times when you should undoubtedly move company, and you may receive offers that are impossible to refuse and come with a promotion. Just remember – wherever you go, there you are. You bring yourself to every move, and if you have not improved your core skills and understanding of what really matters in getting promoted, you may find yourself in exactly the same situation in a new company at the end of your first role with them. Whether you stay or go, my advice is to take the opportunity of working through this book; invest the time now so you understand how promotions work, and invest in yourself to develop proactive skills so that you create an advantage for yourself, whatever you decide.

'It's not fair!' I hear you cry. 'I'm much better than the guy who got promoted.' You might be totally correct. It might be completely unfair, but the way you choose to respond to it is what will define the next stage of your career. It is time to drop any passive-aggressive behaviour in favour of a more strategic approach.

Stop getting in your own way

When passed over for promotion, typically the rejected candidates are given feedback that they are not yet ready for promotion because they lack a specific skill set, or fell short of performance expectations, or they lack the necessary amount of experience for a role promotion – and they may be given quite constructive feedback on what to do to plug the gap. For example, junior managers are often told that they lack the necessary strategic skills to take them to a senior manager position. Sometimes – without any sense of irony – you will be told that you lack experience for the role that you have not yet been given. People looking to be first-time managers are often told that they lack people-management experience.

So how do you square that circle? My advice is to think about what is being said and try to figure out what is being left unsaid, and analyse what may be impeding your promotion. Maybe the feedback-giver is spelling it out perfectly clearly and you need to listen and take it on board. Of course, it is also possible they are not being entirely transparent and honest with you about what is blocking your path, so it is up to you to work it out by taking a fair and frank look at your situation. Perhaps your work performance and results are up to scratch, but there is something else getting in the way of your promotion.

If you can't put your finger on what the issue is, take a look at the following list of typical promotion blockers, and see if any of these factors apply to you. Take this list as an opportunity to identify any personal obstacles. Diagnosing the problem is the first step towards solving it.

The Top Ten Promotion Blockers

1 Lack of confidence

If you want to get promoted, you have to believe in yourself and your potential. Based on all that you have achieved to date, have confidence that you can stretch yourself further to do the next role up. Cut out the negative self-talk. We all feel insecure at times, but if you really want a promotion you have to fully commit and go for it. But don't tip into arrogance. If you get a reputation for being arrogant, then it is quite likely that other people will go out of their way to prevent you from getting promoted. Be confident and assertive, but not arrogant. Confidence in yourself and instilling confidence in the decision-makers is probably the most important currency for securing your next promotion.

2 Poor interpersonal skills

It will not help your promotion chances if you are unfriendly and unpopular with peers, juniors or your boss. Companies and teams are not only about systems, processes and results – they are about people and how they interrelate. When someone does not make an effort to socialize or make small talk with colleagues, it comes across as unfriendly and this may further be interpreted as you not being easy to work with. And if you dominate meetings without regard for other people's views and time, it will not work in your favour outside the meeting. Interpersonal skills matter more than you know. It is easier to get ahead if you make an effort to get on with your peers, your team and others, because it means they are more likely to support your campaign to get promoted.

3 Immaturity

Perhaps you are displaying unhelpful, immature behaviours – and just don't yet have the sophistication for the next level up. For example, maybe you tell jokes in the office that you think are extremely funny, but others find offensive. Ask yourself what behaviour you would expect from top management, and whether you are living up to that standard yourself. Notice what commands respect. Check yourself and try to step up your game in terms of manners and how you behave at work.

4 Entitlement

Some people feel entitled to a promotion based on their own imaginary criteria – such as time served in a role, or age. Perhaps you have been passed over for promotion once, so you feel entitled to the promotion the next time around. Unfortunately it does not work like that. Casting yourself as a victim and complaining about the unfairness of not getting promoted just makes you look entitled rather than deserving. Instead, focus on positive proactive strategies. People will notice and appreciate it all the more if you have a constructive attitude to being passed over. Show you are willing to learn and improve, and to take on board feedback that you are given.

5 Lacking strategic skills

Many people have been told that they lack the necessary strategic skills for the next level up, and it is often said as if that is the end of the matter – as if some people lack a specific strategy gene and can never acquire it. Yet 'strategy' is a technical skill like any other, and it is something you can learn. You can plug that knowledge gap very easily with the right help – if the company won't invest in you, find a strategy development course you can attend at a business school. Start changing your language now to be perceived as more strategic. For example, at your next meeting, when the time is right, ask 'Have we looked at the long-term impact of this situation?' or 'Where do we need to be five years from now, and how do we reset priorities today?' Take opportunities to demonstrate strategic skills by raising questions and issues and finding solutions to do with the longer-term goals of the team and organization, and show you are thinking about the bigger picture and how current plans fit into it.

6 Unwilling to relocate

At some stage in your career, it is likely that a promotion may require you to change location. Try to be flexible and say yes to opportunities that come your way, even when it requires upheaving yourself and your life. If you are ambitious and want that promotion, don't limit yourself to a narrow geographic boundary. Shutting off opportunities can be career-limiting. Perhaps working in your organization's USA headquarters or immersing yourself in an emerging market is exactly the experience you need to take your career to the next level. I appreciate it is challenging to move your life (and family, if that applies) – but before you rule it out, check if the longer-term career opportunity is worth it. Maybe the upheaval of the move could be compensated for in other ways, such as being fast-tracked for the next promotion.

7 Performance issues

The results factor is often what blocks people from getting promoted. You can strategize forever about various tactics regarding how to secure your promotion, and you can talk up your performance all you like – but at the end of the day, if the results are not there, then it will all be in vain. Some people don't put in the effort. Some are clever at blaming their circumstances, other people or any other external factors for poor performance results. In a recession, they blame the recession. When it is not a recession, they find other reasons for non-success – they blame the customer or the team, or the target-setting process. But a pattern of non-results will eventually be impossible to escape. Take responsibility for your performance. Are you really giving 100 per cent in your role?

8 Not trustworthy

It is a major concern if people around you feel you are not loyal to anyone except yourself. You may be getting the right results but be suffering from a trust issue – if you are seen as not loyal to your boss or your colleagues, then this may be what is holding you back from the next-level-up promotion. If you want more responsibility, you have to earn the trust of others so that they feel secure that you can handle it. Don't ever break confidences, and definitely don't engage in gossip about colleagues.

9 Irreplaceable in current role

Ironically, you may be getting in your own way by being too good in your current role. Irreplaceable people cannot be promoted; it may be too inconvenient for your boss and everyone else if you were moved to another role. For example, perhaps the company is concerned that a key client relationship may suffer if a promotion meant you had to move to a bigger customer account. To counteract this kind of challenge, you may have to identify and train up your own successor, and insist when they are ready to take over. If you seem content to be excelling in this role, and you don't push for the next role, your boss may be quite happy to keep you *in situ*.

10 Misalignment with your boss

Try to keep the relationship between you and your manager running smoothly day to day. You might be surprised at how jarring your boss finds your daily habits if they are totally opposite to theirs – and how this may negatively affect their perception of you. Perhaps your boss is a neat freak and you have a constantly untidy desk. Or they come in early, and you are always late. If it's not too difficult for you, try to mirror your boss's daily habits so that you are more in sync and so you don't irritate your boss unnecessarily. For your own sake, don't be too argumentative or challenging for your boss, to the point that they find you annoying.

It's not me, it's my boss!

Eve didn't get on with her boss, and took no responsibility for her part in this deteriorating relationship. Eve was convinced her boss was the problem, and decided the answer was to leave the company. She joined another interesting company – she worked in the technology industry, so it was relatively easy to move around. But after the honeymoon of the first three months was over, she was in conflict with her new boss too. 'I'm so unlucky,' Eve said to herself. After less than two years of conflict with her new boss, Eve decided it was too stressful to stay and decided to leave the company.

Without any self-insight, the scenario played out again and again and again. Eve felt sorry for herself that she always picked the 'wrong' boss – and concluded that bosses had a problem with her because she was so good that they felt threatened by her. Eve should have realized that the pattern showed that she had the problem, not her bosses. That perhaps she was being arrogant and just didn't like having a boss, because she thought she knew better than them.

Well, unless your boss's boss agrees – or you're going to start up your own business – you are always going to have a boss, and you need to respect them and find a way to get on with them.

Consider whether any of these promotion blockers apply to your situation, and think what you can do about it. If you are getting in your own way, the good news is that you can evolve and change. If any of the above hit a nerve, then consider it good news – because if you can put your finger on exactly what the problem is, then your focus can switch to solving that problem and you are a step closer to getting promoted.

Am I getting in the way of my promotion?	✓ Yes	✗ No
Lack of confidence		
Poor interpersonal skills		
Immaturity		
Entitlement		
Lacking strategic skills		
Unwilling to relocate		
Performance issues		
Not trustworthy		
Irreplaceable in current role		˘
Misalignment with your boss		

Don't expect your work to speak for itself

It is not enough to do great work. People have to know about it too! It is not something that everyone is comfortable doing, but learning to publicize your achievements is the key to getting promoted. You will need to have the confidence to speak up, share your progress and get the credit you deserve.

We like to believe that people have noticed our diligent work and recognize our potential – but in the sometimes over-whelming busy-ness of all that needs to be achieved at work, it is better to assume that no one has the time to go and search out your greatness. Silently waiting to be noticed and not self-advocating has the potential to be misconstrued as having nothing to say for yourself. You need to publicize your work to key stakeholders in order to get the recognition you deserve. This may feel uncomfortable to start with – especially if you think of yourself as an introvert. But there will always be a noisy extrovert around who will make a big show of their ideas. Your results and qualities are valuable, and you have to make sure they don't go unnoticed. Always seek to make construct-ive, substance-based contributions. Share credit for accom-plishments with those who helped you.

Give yourself the best possible shot at promotion with the following actions:

✓ Be your own publicist

✓ Speak up regularly at meetings

✓ Have more presence and impact

✓ Raise the energy level of your contributions

✓ Grow your resilience

Be your own publicist

Record your accomplishments and showcase these regularly to your boss and others. Unless you explain the obstacles you had to overcome, they will simply assume that you had a straight-forward time of it. They will be more impressed when you ex-plain what you wanted to achieve, the challenges that faced you, the effort involved and the creative solutions you found to problems. Don't shy away from taking your turn at the meeting to update co-workers on your progress. Connect your work to the bigger picture and the overall strategy; explain why your piece of the puzzle matters. At a minimum, people like to hear what others are doing – sometimes, new synergies will be discovered.

Speak up regularly at meetings

Share your opinion with your boss and with your colleagues at team meetings, backed up by the conclusions you have drawn from your own work and experiences. Let people know what you think. You have a point of view that is unique and refreshing and helpful. Perhaps what you say today will unlock a problem your company or team is facing, because you bring a different perspective to the situation. Don't assume that other people automatically know better than you. Empower yourself to speak up and get involved, even when you feel trepidation about speaking in the group.

TOP TIP

If you work remotely, stay visible

Unfortunately, remote workers can suffer from being 'out of sight, out of mind'. When you are not usually present in the office, you need to be even more conscious of speaking up and showcasing your work online. Schedule regular online meetings with your boss and key stakeholders. Stay within their literal sight lines. Contribute regularly at meetings. Take the lead on new projects. Stay connected, and don't let your remote-working situation become a barrier to securing your next promotion.

Have more presence and impact

Don't rely on your routine day-to-day contributions as your only means of making an impact. Offer to set the agenda of the next meeting – and take the opportunity to give a presentation on your progress or your team's accomplishments. Reach for something more to say or do to showcase your work. Use the full suite of social media platforms and technology tools available to you. Become a regular contributor on LinkedIn, or make use of Twitter or Instagram to get your work noticed. Having 'presence' is often about confidently doing the opposite of what everyone else is doing or what you are expected to do. For example, in the midst of a crisis, rather than getting lost in the drama, be the one who stays very calm and makes constructive suggestions about next steps. Stand up to stand out. When everyone else is sitting down at the meeting, be the one to stand up when you are talking.

Raise the energy level of your contributions

It's not just what you say, it's how you say it that gets you noticed. Obviously, no mumbling! Speak up and speak clearly. Use emotion and your tone of voice to make your presentations more energetic and more exciting to listen to. Perhaps you could open with a shock statement about the conclusion, to get everyone's attention – for example, 'We have been ignoring our customers!' Or start by asking a question – 'What if we did it another way?!' – and then, having secured the attention of the room, start your presentation.

When you raise your personal energy level, you help raise the energy of the room. Play around with energy levels to see what works, and how far you can push it without overdoing it. Next time you enter a low-energy meeting where everyone is troubled by a problem, rather than be dragged down by the low mood of others, switch it up with some high-energy questions so that you inspire people to rethink the problem. 'What could we do differently?' 'Where are the green shoots?' 'What does this situation remind us of, and what lesson did we learn back then?' 'Who else can help us?'

Grow your resilience

Lean in to any fears you may have that, by putting your views forward, you might embarrass yourself or someone might belittle your opinion or your meeting contribution. Expect it to happen sometimes, and don't retire back into your shell when it does. Just explain why you came to your conclusions. When you don't make the impact you want, just shrug it off and try again next time with another contribution. Be reasonably robust when putting forward your ideas, and be prepared to defend them. Usually the people who put other people down are very insecure themselves, and you should see their put-downs as indications of their own lack of confidence and carry on being confident yourself. Just do your best. Sometimes you'll succeed, sometimes you'll fail. Don't dwell too much on either the successes or the failures. Everything is an experience that we learn from. Just keep moving forward.

2   Empower yourself

Take charge and get organized

The best way to approach the task of getting promoted is to see it as a new project alongside your day job. This is helpful for a couple of reasons: first, it means you realize that you need to dedicate time and effort that is separate to your day-to-day work; and second, because it reinforces the fact that just doing a great job in your current role is not enough. Trying to secure a promotion is not business as usual. It requires additional energy and focus. Carve out enough time to invest in making this new project a success.

My advice is to start by putting two hours a week aside to concentrate on your get-promoted project, using this book as a guide. Use the get-promoted game plan described in the next chapter to work out what you need to do to ensure you have covered all bases.

Within a few weeks, as you become more familiar with the concepts, the get-promoted effort will start to permeate your daily thinking and behaviours – and it will become more integrated into your mindset and approach at work. But you should still take the time to step back and consider how much progress (or not) you are making. To get a better perspective, try to locate yourself outside the office physically when you are reviewing your progress and strategizing about your promotion and career – this will help you look at things more objectively. Consider finding a supportive internal mentor too, or hire an external coach to give you extra impetus. A mentor could be someone more senior and experienced in your organization who is willing to help you navigate the culture at work, and support you with wise advice. An executive coach won't have the inside track on how your company's system works, but they are professionally qualified and trained to challenge your assumptions about yourself and your company, and can help you gain a fresh perspective.

Like everything else you want to achieve in life, promotion is about 'energy in, energy out'. In other words, the more effort you put into the task, the faster you will achieve the outcome you desire. Don't wait until a couple of months prior to the company's next annual promotion round to set up your get-promoted project and plan. You need to take a much more proactive approach that is about breaking free of the rules – both real and perceived. You can even be the exception that gets promoted during the year, rather than at the end of the year. Stop waiting for others to determine your future, and start creating opportunities for yourself. Begin your get-promoted project this week, and by the time it is up and running – and you are regularly applying the concepts found in this book – you will be pleasantly surprised at how much faster you will get results.

Understand your current environment

A good place to start with your get-promoted project is to take stock of your current situation. Here are a few questions you can ask yourself to get a clearer picture of whether your environment is structurally set up to support promotion opportunities, or whether you should think about moving to a better environment:

- **How much competition is there?**

  My advice will help you compete for promotion no matter how much competition there is. However, it is undoubtedly easier to get promoted into a role that has three interested candidates versus three hundred. Are there ways that you could reduce the volume of competition for your next promotion? For example, would there be less competition if you moved towards a niche speciality or into a brand-new market opportunity? Understanding the supply and demand for more senior roles at your company will offer a reality check in terms of just how much you may need to raise your game to differentiate yourself from the competition.

- **How successful is your company?**

  If your company is profitable and thriving, then they are in a better position to offer new opportunities. Global corporate brands usually have plenty of scope for new roles and promotions, both locally and internationally. Many consulting firms have well-trodden graduate programmes and talent management fast-track programmes. Tech industry start-ups are examples of high-growth companies – where the whole business model and mission requires that they scale fast and take the company public. Do you belong to a growing company? Is your company in a strong and stable position to support your desired future promotions, or do you need to consider moving to a better environment?

- **How supportive is your boss?**
  Ideally, you have a boss who is invested in your success and wants you to reach your full potential. When your boss is supportive, you have a higher chance of getting promoted. Consider your boss for a moment – do you think they understand that it is part of their job to make sure you're doing your best work and that you're constantly developing your skill set so you are ready to move on to the next stage of your career? Would your boss consider you as their successor? Try to open up a conversation with your boss about their own career path, to understand more about where they see themselves going next, and when – and whether in that context they would have any plans to take you with them, or have you succeed them.

If you already operate in an environment which has one or more of these structural advantages in place, that is great news for you. The next stage of your get-promoted plan will be all about making the most of it. But for some of you, asking these questions will clarify that the odds are not stacked in your favour. You may need to think about a lateral move to a new boss or work environment. This doesn't always mean you need to leave your company – it could be a strategic move to another division. Whatever your situation, my advice can help you – even against all the odds – but it is better for you to have your eyes wide open and understand the role your current context plays in hampering or determining your ability to move forward. When you appreciate the size of the challenge, you can be more strategic and thoughtful about whether a smart move to another boss or another part of your company – or even leaving your company altogether – is the key to further progress.

Whatever your situation, you must take charge of the path

towards your next promotion. Don't put your career in the hands of someone else. If you joined a corporate organization as a graduate hire, you may have been inducted in a very organized and streamlined way. Most companies hire graduates in bulk numbers, and have become very good at the induction resources necessary for supporting graduates in making a successful transition from unstructured campus life to a more structured work environment. If this was your experience, don't allow it to lull you into a false sense of security and think that this level of expert induction and support will continue throughout your career. I remember when I joined a management consultancy as a graduate, our career paths were thoroughly attended to for five years until we became managers, and then – suddenly – it was every man and woman for herself, cut adrift in a sink-or-swim, competitive pyramid structure.

Your boss is likely to be extremely busy or even overwhelmed by the amount of responsibility and work on their plate. They don't always have the time to invest in carefully considering your career happiness and next moves. They prefer you to take responsibility for yourself. Bosses value people who take initiative and proactively manage their own careers, rather than expecting someone else to 'parent' them. If most of your peers are 'needy' and waiting to be taken care of, you can automatically set yourself apart by having a proactive career plan and taking charge of creating your own forward path. What boss wouldn't like an employee who is proactive and determined and ambitious? Be that person. Don't wait around for your career to be managed – manage it yourself.

Remember, you are not just competing with your peers for the next role, you are also competing with jobseekers from outside the firm – and you can be sure that they are dedicating time and effort to polishing up their CVs, meeting new people and talking up their accomplishments. Internal people are often very disgruntled when an outsider becomes their boss – as they understand nothing of the culture and all the tacit knowledge that you possess. It feels so unfair, but you need to accept the reasons why an outsider may be a more attractive option – they bring new energy, new ideas, a different and fresh perspective. Think about what you can do to counteract this 'threat' and find ways to compete by continuing to refresh and reinvent yourself.

Perhaps you could recreate the same advantages of being an external hire, or by moving to a different division or team within your current company. Or ideate on what action you could take to gain more relevant knowledge and experience and reposition yourself within your current role and company. This might mean taking a week off to do an executive education course, or agreeing on a three-month job swap in another part of the business.

Specific advice for women and minority groups

The advice in this book applies equally to everyone. However, the odds of success may be more stacked against you if you belong to a minority group in your organization, because you may be overlooked for promotion due to overt or unconscious bias by decision-makers.

Unconscious biases are learned stereotypes that are automatic, unintentional and deeply ingrained, and left unchecked they can negatively influence recruitment and promotion decisions. Fortunately, society and workplaces are improving, and many organizations are more educated on the need for diversity and inclusion, and the importance of surfacing and eliminating unconscious biases – but the playing field is not yet level.

You may also have internalized some of that societal and workplace bias. For example, some women may need to pay conscious attention to overcoming a tendency to undersell accomplishments. Some women are less assertive in meetings if they don't have perfect data, versus men who make confident assertions based on less data or even a hunch. When resources are scarce, some women may be compliant with organizational requests to do more with less, while men might still elbow their way into any available resources.

So how do you break free of any limits being placed on you by others, or any limits you place on yourself? My advice is to empower yourself as a person whose uniqueness and difference brings a compelling and invaluable perspective. Embolden yourself with the knowledge that diversity is not only an equality imperative, but a critical strategy for business and leadership success. Know that people from diverse backgrounds expand innovation and are great problem-solvers because they bring a fresh approach.

TOP TIP FOR PARENTS

Give clear signals about whether you are in the fast or the slow lane

A word of advice to mothers and fathers who signal that they want to move into the 'slow lane' at work while their children are young – it is critical that you signal when you are ready to move back into the fast lane.

The slow-lane signals may be when you let your boss know that you are reluctant to take on any extra responsibility for a period of time, due to juggling work and home priorities. If you do this, don't expect your boss to assume you ever want to get back into the fast lane. They may have written you off for new promotion opportunities, and you need to keep them up to speed on when you are ready for more responsibility or will consider relocating. If you don't communicate this, further promotion opportunities will not even be presented to you because the boss thinks you are not up for it – and they won't even give you the chance to discuss it and consider the benefits for you and your family.

You may not even have realized that you gave out slow-lane signalling. So if you feel like your career has stagnated and you are not sure why, talk to your boss about your ambitions. If your boss is surprised to hear that you want a promotion and more responsibility, then unfortunately you have been sending out the wrong signals, and you need to accept this and rectify the situation as soon as possible by being clearer in your communication and making sure your actions back up your desire for promotion.

3 Your get-promoted game plan

Six key moves to get promoted

It is helpful to deconstruct the bigger challenge of how to get promoted into distinct moves. Each of these has its own impact – and combined, their impact is maximized. Breaking down your game plan into steps makes the challenge more approachable and less intimidating, and you can focus on each component in turn. This will create positive momentum.

With this in mind, I have deconstructed the get-promoted game plan into six key moves. I describe the whole plan here, and subsequently devote a whole chapter to each step.

| Figure 1: Your Get-Promoted Game Plan

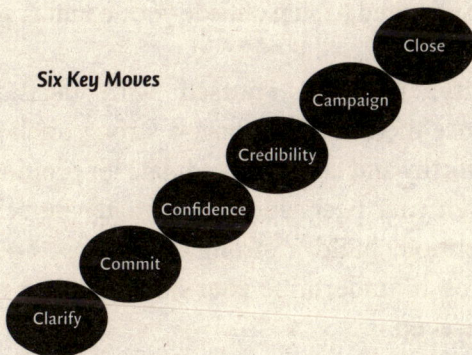

Six Key Moves

Close

Campaign

Credibility

Confidence

Commit

Clarify

Clarify: Before launching into your promotion plan, step back and look at the bigger picture. What do you want from your career? Why do you want to get promoted? How does your next step fit in with your long-term career goals? Understand what is really motivating you. Identify or create the promotion opportunity you seek. Establish who makes the promotion decision.

Commit: Be prepared to put in the work. You will need to work hard not just on your day job, but also on your get-promoted project. You need to carve out time and invest energy in following the ideas I outline in this book. Put yourself forward and ask for the promotion. Be ready to learn, grow and change. Since all promotions ultimately result in a leadership position, you should fully commit and start behaving like a leader now.

Confidence: You may really want the promotion, but are you truly confident that you can do that step-up role? Belief in your own abilities and potential is critical if you want others to believe in you. This is about appreciating your strengths and the value you would bring to the new role. You may need to build your confidence, tackle imposter syndrome and be prepared to step outside your comfort zone.

Credibility: Establish yourself with decision-makers. Convince them that you have a strong track record and are a worthy and credible candidate for promotion. Stand out from your peers and differentiate yourself from the competition, build a strong reputation, and don't do anything to undermine your credibility for roles at the next level up.

Campaign: Develop a groundswell of support around you. You need to figure out who the decision-makers and influencers are in the decision to promote you. Your boss may not be the sole decision-maker – in fact, they may have nothing to do with the decision. By understanding the different stakeholders, you can think more carefully about how to manage them. A great promotion campaign incorporates an understanding of company politics and culture, harnesses influence and momentum, and shows substance underpinning why you should be the chosen candidate, in the form of a First 100 Days plan and a pitch for the role.

Close: Figure out how to close the deal. Even when you have been promised a promotion, there may be work required to bring it over the line, such as formalizing a new title, negotiating your pay and terms, and agreeing your start date. Part of the closing phase may also involve deciding whether or not to turn down a promotion if it is not actually the role you want, or the terms are not what you want. You may be wondering what to do if no 'right' promotions ever come your way.

When you have familiarized yourself with these moves, it might be of further help to write up your get-promoted game plan with goals for each key move and set a timeline in which to achieve them – an immediate first step, things to do within three months, then six months, then a year. Giving yourself a timeline for outcomes will give you an added impetus and also provide a useful framework against which you can measure your progress. For example, at the three-month milestone, re-flect back on what progress you have made, what is working or not working in relation to your efforts, and reset your agenda and priorities for the next three months.

The *Get Promoted* '3-6-12' Template

	KEY MILESTONES			
6 KEY MOVES	First Step Actions	Goals by end of 3 months	Goals by end of 6 months	Goals by end of 12 months
On Clarify				
On Commit				
On Confidence				
On Credibility				
On Campaign				
On Close				

Although I am describing your get-promoted game plan as if it is a linear process to be fully completed, don't get overly rigid about the process and your path to promotion. Be open-minded about fresh opportunities that may arise faster than expected. By investing time and effort in securing your next promotion, a new momentum is created and people may start to notice you and your capability. Your more proactive attitude and approach may mean you are offered interesting and unexpected opportunities. When life offers you a great opportunity, grab it! As you change, new possibilities will open up. For example, you may suddenly be given extra responsibility for an important special project, which gives you more visibility with senior stakeholders, which puts you in a better position for a future promotion. One success leads to another.

Now let's examine each of those six moves in more detail.

4   Clarify

What is really motivating you?

What is driving your ambition for promotion? It may be helpful to think about your long-term career goals and short-term
promotion desires by considering extrinsic and intrinsic motivations, and thinking about what is driving you.

Extrinsic and intrinsic motivations influence our behaviour, consciously and unconsciously. Extrinsic motivations
arise from external influences, like seeking prestige or more
pay or wanting to impress other people. Intrinsic motivations
are internal drivers that touch deeper chords within us, such
as our core values and what is truly at stake for us in the pursuit of what really matters to us. Although extrinsic motivations are powerful, and certainly you need a certain amount
of financial reward to pursue a good life, these external motivations cannot by themselves lead to internal satisfaction for
most people.

Considering how much time we all invest in work, it makes
more sense that we should prioritize intrinsic motivations and
strive to feel connected to and have a sense of purpose about
our work. Rather than rushing forward with your get-promoted
strategy, thinking only of the promotion right in front of you,
take some time to consider what truly matters to you – and

| **Figure 2: Intrinsic and extrinsic motivations**

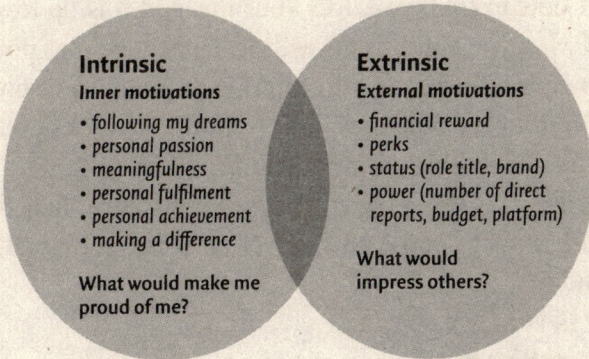

Intrinsic
Inner motivations
- *following my dreams*
- *personal passion*
- *meaningfulness*
- *personal fulfilment*
- *personal achievement*
- *making a difference*

What would make me proud of me?

Extrinsic
External motivations
- *financial reward*
- *perks*
- *status (role title, brand)*
- *power (number of direct reports, budget, platform)*

What would impress others?

why. The obvious next step on your current career path might not be the right next step in terms of making you happy. If this reflection on what really matters to you changes your career ambitions and offers a reframe on your dream job and what role would set you on that path, then you have saved yourself years – and potentially a wasted career.

You don't have to follow the career path set out by your company. Taking time to reassess now will help you decide what you really want to achieve with all the time and energy you invest in your work life, and you can redirect your focus to those ambitions. If you can tap into your inner motivations for why you want something, then it's more likely that you will stay motivated and keep trying for it – and while you are striving and when you get promoted, you will feel more personally fulfilled. Intrinsic motivation keeps you energized to dig deeper and persevere, so you can achieve your goals in the face of any challenges along the way. If you can truly identify and connect with what drives you intrinsically, then all your energy, intentions and decisions will be aligned in a positive direction – and you are more likely to achieve personal and professional success.

Don't expect your company, your boss or anyone else to figure out how to fulfil you. It is your life, and it is up to you to decide what you want to do with it. Don't give that power to other people – they can't truly know your inner life or how you wish to fulfil your potential. Take responsibility for developing yourself and working out what you need and want.

Be ambitious, think big and find your purpose. Take the opportunity now to pause and reflect on what really matters to you, and why.

What matters to me?

Personally	Professionally
Examples:	Examples:
Make a difference, and have an impact	Fulfil my leadership potential
Create a better world for my children	Unleash the potential of others
Show others that they shouldn't have underestimated me	Use my talents, skills and knowledge
	Reach the top of my profession
Feel pride in my achievements – make my parents proud!	Become the global expert
	Mastery of a skill area
A journey of self-discovery – what am I capable of achieving if I truly commit?	Expand my reputation
	Leave a professional legacy
Get to the top fast, retire early, pursue a 'second act' career or other broader interests	
Financial freedom	

Having thought more broadly about what really matters to you, put your next promotion in the context of what you want to achieve long-term with your career. Think about the following questions:

- Do you know what you want to achieve long-term in your career?

- Will this next promotion serve you well for future ambitions?

- Does it put you on the right path to pursue your ultimate career goals?

- Is it an interesting and fulfilling role, regardless of the possibilities of where it may take you next?

- Are you pursuing a particular career track for status, money or power only – and is it time to step back and completely rethink what you want from your career and next role?

It is possible to be successful, well paid, enjoy your work, and leave a positive legacy behind for the benefit of other people. There don't necessarily have to be trade-offs. You can have it all – as long as you are clear on what 'having it all' actually means to you. Don't abandon long-term personal fulfilment in pursuit of a short-term flattering promotion.

Start with the end in mind, and think about what career legacy you want to leave behind. Do you want to change the world, improve the planet, make a difference to other people, build a company, become a world-class expert, become the CEO? Ask yourself:

- What do I really care about?

- What is my ultimate dream role?

- How does my next promotion fit in?

Then think about:

- What are my core values? What do I believe in?

- What are my passions and interests?

- Who inspires me?

- What brings me joy?

- When do I feel most fulfilled at work?

The more clarity you have on what drives you and your vision of career success, the faster you can achieve that success – because all your energy will be focused on the next steps. Having crystal-clear intentions in terms of future outcomes will fuel you to unleash all your talents and effort to achieve your mission – starting with your next desired promotion.

Identify or create the promotion opportunity

With more clarity about the bigger picture and what matters to you, you can use formal networks like your HR department or your boss to identify existing or upcoming role vacancies. But how are you going to set about creating the promotion opportunity if the right role vacancy is not immediately in front of you? Perhaps the current holder of your desired next role has no plans to leave the position for another five years, or has no prospective job to move on to. Maybe you are not available to be moved right now, because you are midway through a critical project or deliverable – which means that your boss will not relinquish you from your current role for another year or two. If you consider that, typically, most roles are for three years only, have a think about the rhythms of the role you hold and the role you desire, and how the timings could play out and align.

So what can you do to create opportunity for promotion?

Get your successor ready

Is there someone ready to take over your current role? As previously mentioned, one barrier to your promotion could be that you are indispensable. Getting a very competent replacement lined up helps to make your manager's work life as easy as possible, and removes that blocker to getting yourself promoted. My advice is that you should start thinking about succession as soon as you arrive in a role.

Anticipate role rhythms

For the role you are interested in, find out how long the present incumbent has been in place. If they have only moved into that role within the past twelve months, then realistically it won't be available for a couple of years. Think about what you could do in the meantime to gain more experience and position yourself as the ideal successor for that role – or is there another role promotion you should aim for instead?

Craft a new role

Think about how to pitch a bespoke next-level-up role that plays to your strengths – and which doesn't exist in your structure right now. Because you will be the one who came up with the idea, you will have automatically eliminated any competition. Chief Operating Officer, Chief of Staff, Special Projects Manager and Head of Strategic Innovation are great roles to propose if they don't already exist. Such titles can be established and defined according to your strengths, and could be negotiated to come with a promotion.

Step up within your team

See if you can promote yourself into a deputy role within your team by ideating such a role with your boss, which will simultaneously take the burden of some specific projects and responsibilities off them. If it can't come with a promotion immediately, it could be part of a two-step fast-track process. If you can be seen as a first among equals, it makes it more credible that you will be the one to secure a promotion next. It is a clever way to secure your promotion in advance.

Chief your current role

Make your current role more strategic by reframing it with a more strategic title. I worked with an HR director to re-platform her role as 'Chief People Officer', which secured her a role promotion and a position at the executive committee management meetings. The title change was about demonstrating her capability to come up with new ideas on people matters, and showcasing why her contributions would be valued at those meetings. If 'Chief' is a step too far, what about putting 'Senior' in front of your current role?

Stay alert to moves and opportunities

Be alert when someone is about to retire, or when you know that someone is interviewing externally (i.e. about to create a vacancy when they leave), or when someone at the next level up announces their pregnancy and their role needs temporary cover (which would give you a step-up opportunity to prove your worth at that level for other roles). Notice when your boss is complaining about the burden of their responsibilities, as it might be an opportunity to suggest you take some of those responsibilities from them.

Get ahead of organization change

Be alert to upcoming changes in the top leadership group and major restructures like a new CEO being appointed, new strategic initiatives, or any other significant organization change. It is also worth keeping an eye on how the sector and economy more generally are faring, to anticipate any changes. A new CEO will inevitably reshuffle their leadership team. What implications will that have for your boss and for you? How might the new CEO shift the strategic agenda – and how could you find out more about that, and anticipate probable structural reorganization and potential new roles?

For proactive people who manage their careers strategically, an organization restructure is not something to be feared. It is an opportunity to progress by finding out why the restructure is happening, what new roles may emerge, and trying to align accordingly with what is needed to support the new strategic direction.

Volunteer for a strategy task force

From time to time a company will initiate a cross-functional strategy task force to look at the long-term prospects of the business and assess its organizational fitness to deliver. They may require employee help to research and analyse trends and possible future scenarios, and to contribute ideas on how the company may need to respond and reorganize accordingly. You need to get on that strategy task force! It is the inside scoop on what is coming down the track in terms of potential future roles and strategic priorities.

Consider who could help you

Try to meet people outside your division and in headquarters, to find out what is going on elsewhere in the organization. Think about who you already know that is now in a position of seniority or influence. Suggest coffee with them. The best way to gather information is an informal meet-up with any highly connected people, on the basis that they might know of organization changes or role vacancies, existing or coming up. Think back to a great boss you had in the past who may be sympathetic and willing to help you progress in your career. Meet up with anyone you know who always seems to have the inside track on things.

Taking advantage of the 'guilt' opportunity

When you have just been passed over for a promotion, there is a window of time following a decision not to appoint you when the decision-makers and influencers feel guilty that you invested in a process and were turned down. This is perfect timing to ask for something extra!

I started working with a client who had just been turned down by the CEO for the divisional leadership role on his team. My client had personally invested in getting ready for the role – even relocating his family to the USA a few years earlier in anticipation (and with encouragement from the CEO, who needed him in America at the time). When the final appointment did not pan out accordingly, I intuited that the CEO must surely feel very guilty.

I suggested to my client that he propose a new role on the CEO's executive leadership team with the title Chief Operating Officer (COO). The types of responsibilities the COO could be tasked with were special objectives and projects which would alleviate the pressure of the CEO role. It created a win–win situation: my client could still get a promotion, step up and participate as a member of the executive leadership team; and the CEO got an extra pair of hands and didn't need to feel guilty any more. This was about being creative and taking advantage of timing and emotion, and it worked!

Establish who makes the decision

Work out who really makes the decision on who gets appointed for your desired next role. Think about all the stakeholders involved in the promotion decision, and categorize them as either decision-makers or influencers. This is helpful because it will focus your campaign effort accordingly.

For internal promotions within the same team or department, most people assume their boss makes the promotion decision, but that is not always the case. Sometimes it will be your boss's boss – and your boss's boss may be mostly influenced by the HR advisor. So you might need to cast your net a bit further than the obvious when thinking about the key stakeholders involved in the promotion/appointment decision. If you desire a promotion in another division or team, then your boss's view of you will still be important – but only as an influencer.

For any prospective promotion, consider the following:

- Who would be your 'hard reporting line' (direct) boss?

- Who, if anyone, would be your 'dotted reporting line' (indirect) boss/es?

- Which HR people/advisors are likely to be involved?

- How much influence will your current boss have on the decision?

- How much influence will your peers, team and customers (present and future) have on the decision?

- Who will be in the room when the final promotion decision is made?

The main priority of your get-promoted campaign will be to build a relationship with the decision-makers; and very often when you take out all the people who belong in the influencer category, there is only one decision-maker. Nine times out of ten, the 'hard line' boss for the role you desire is the final decision-maker – because they have the most at stake in terms of who should be put in the role, and whether it works out or not in the longer term. The rest are then influencers.

You need to focus on convincing the decision-maker. However, don't underestimate the power of key influencers. Some organizations, for promotions at some levels, have a system of group decision-making. In those situations, you need to figure out who will be in the room when the final decision on your promotion is made. When influencers are in the room, they have more proximate power – and this means they can exert extra pressure on the decision-maker in the final stages.

When I take on a new client, I ask them, 'Who is the one person who could insist that you are appointed and no one would object?' and then we focus on building the relationship with that person. I once worked with a client who wanted a promotion to group Chief Strategy Officer. He was initially very concerned with all the stakeholders and their view of him for the role. I pointed out that only the group CEO made this particular role decision, and since my client had a peripheral relationship with the group CEO, then that was where his campaign effort needed to focus. You shouldn't have endless amounts of people on your stakeholder list and miss the bigger picture. Don't overanalyse. Sometimes the simplest answer is the one that cuts through.

With another client, who thought her boss would make the decision, I asked if she had a relationship with her boss's boss. She had never invested in forming one. I suggested to her that if her boss's boss was very impressed with her, he could potentially override her boss and anyone else in the decision-making or influence chain. And she agreed that if her boss's boss insisted, then she would be appointed. So we focused on her boss's boss. When he needed someone to tour customer sites with him, she immediately volunteered, and she invested time in impressing him with her knowledge and the depth of her customer relationships – during preparation for the event, the tour itself and in the follow-up notes afterwards. When it came to making the promotion decision, the boss's boss wanted her appointed and that was that. She had earned the promotion, but as I will never tire of saying, it doesn't matter that you have done the hard work – you also need to let the key people know who you are and what you have achieved! When she got the promotion, she thanked me and said that it would never have occurred to her to take the opportunity to volunteer and build a relationship with her boss's boss. In the end, one creative suggestion can be what seals the deal.

But sometimes, no matter what you do, your promotion will be blocked by strong influencers who have made it their mission to stop your appointment going ahead. There are politics in every decision, and sometimes negative forces will work against you. If your detractors spot a weakness in your approach or you have gained a poor reputation for any reason, then this will be used against you by a strong negative influencer. You need to be alert to this reality and be ready to manage the politics of your situation. Politics in decision-making become increasingly complex as you become more senior and there is more competition for fewer positions. The good news is that politics is a skill, and you can learn how to navigate the politics of your promotion. I devote a whole section in chapter 8 to how to develop a great get-promoted campaign.

5   Commit

Ask for the promotion

Progressing in your career is about having a proactive strategy and taking action once you have ideas on how to move forward. Wishing for the promotion you desire and committing to securing it are two entirely different mindsets. You need to fully commit to doing what it takes. Decide now that you are fully dedicated not just to the idea of getting promoted but to putting yourself out there – and that includes having the courage to ask.

'If you don't ask, you won't get' certainly applies to promotions. Many people wait to be noticed and tapped on the shoulder. They expect others to take charge of their career, to support them, to spot their potential. This strategy is fine when you are a graduate or in the early years of your career, when there are more clearly laid-out routes to manager level and many middle management vacancies to fill. However, the structure of an organization is typically pyramid-shaped and narrows ever more tightly towards the top, so sitting back and waiting is not going to get you ahead of the competition. In such a competitive work environment, where there are far more people than roles available – and there is the possibility of fresh talent being hired in from outside each year – you can't wait to be noticed and promoted. You have to fully commit, put yourself forward and ask for what you want.

It sounds like very obvious advice, doesn't it, to ask for the promotion you want – and for many of you, it is as straightforward as that. But I also recognize how difficult it can be, because of a fear of rejection. Don't be afraid to be told 'no', or 'not yet'. Reframe any 'rejection' as a learning opportunity, and ask for constructive feedback on what it might take for you to secure the role in the future. It is better to ask and find out what others think of you, than waste time not knowing and not being able to work on areas that are causing decision-makers to doubt you. Believe in yourself; have the courage of your convictions. Be clear and committed to the task at hand, and ask for the promotion you want. Sometimes people assume that, because it is obvious to them that they would want a promotion, then it should be obvious to everyone else. Actually, decision-makers are just as likely to conclude you do not especially want the promotion if you have not made the effort to ask for it – especially if they are under more pressure from another candidate who is showing that desire.

Of course, it helps to know the right way to ask.

| Figure 3: How to ask

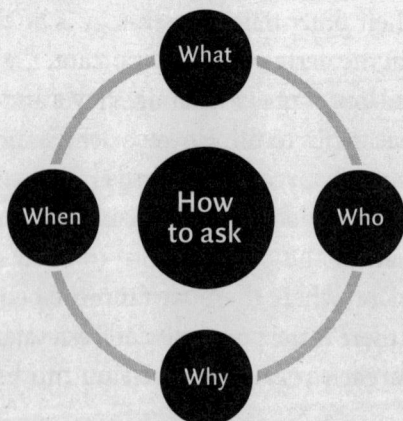

What: Be specific about your role promotion request –
include the role level, title and time frame. Just asking for
a generic promotion without a specific new role definition
and stepped-up responsibilities is too vague. It sounds
like you just want advancement for its own sake, without
seeing the bigger picture of how this promotion fits in with
your career path and how it aligns with the organization's
needs.

Who: List the promotion influencers and decision-makers,
and identify who the ultimate decision-maker is. Remember, it may not be your current boss or your prospective new
boss. The ultimate decision-maker is usually either the most
senior person involved or the person who has most at
stake in terms of the candidate's success in the role.

Why: State your case on why the promotion matters to you,
why you are the best person for the job, and – crucially –
why it would benefit the company. Speak up with energy
and passion, as you are more likely to secure the position
if the decision-maker believes you are truly motivated to
step up and do a great job.

When: Timing, as always, is very important. Ask the decision-
maker at a time when you think they are most receptive
to the request. This might be when your team or department
hits its annual target, or after a significant personal
triumph such as closing a major sales deal or win for the
company, or just after you have received great customer
praise and feedback. Be alert to when you think the
decision-maker is feeling particularly benevolent – another
example might be when the decision-maker has just had

some personal success of their own. Pick your moment wisely. It is usually much better to clearly indicate your intentions ahead of time, so you don't catch your manager unaware. Give them a chance to think it over rather than risk them feeling backed into a corner if you go for the element of surprise in a meeting. When you push for an answer too fast, you may be more likely to get a 'no' than a 'yes'.

TOP TIP

Start talking about your dream role

If your dream role is at least two or three steps away, then start talking about that dream role now. Start building your support base, and take steps towards that goal. This gives you an opportunity to sense-check whether there is any credibility (from those around you) in your potential to do that role. When you ask senior leaders for advice on what it would take to secure that dream role, you are killing two birds with one stone – in effect, you are putting yourself forward as a future candidate for that position, and you are figuring out the roadmap for how to go about securing it. Both of these things will push you further in the direction of that desired role. Sometimes the act of asking is what gives others the confidence that you believe in yourself, and this encourages them that you can do the role.

Usually the asking is not a one-off conversation – it will involve a number of follow-ups after your initial request. See it as a series of conversations rather than thinking of it as a simple 'yes' or 'no'. By asking the first time, you plant the seed, but you then have to nurture the seed and let it grow in the mind of the decision-maker, and reinforce it with all your positive get-promoted strategies.

You could plant the seed by asking in a constructive way, such as 'What would it take for me to get promoted to the next level by the end of the year?' It could become the basis for a series of career-mentoring conversations where you get the decision-maker or key influencers on your side and batting for you, giving them the feeling that they are part of your success when the promotion is attained.

How to ask

David was in middle management. He was very ambitious and keen to secure a promotion to Chief Strategy Officer. The post already had someone in the role, so the vacancy did not exist yet, and it was unclear how long the role-holder would be staying in that job. Rather than wait to be noticed, David decided he would put himself forward for the role anyway. 'Nothing ventured, nothing gained,' he thought. 'If I don't put myself forward, how will anyone know I'm interested?'

What: Chief Strategy Officer

Who: The decision-maker was the Chief Executive Officer; the role reported to him and he had most at stake. The influencers were the other leaders who currently reported to the CEO.

Why: David would have to make the case that it would be beneficial to the CEO and company to promote him – because of his strategic skills, his impetus and energy, and his fresh ideas for creating a better future for the organization and its customers. David knew the CSO role played to his strengths and would be a stepping stone to his eventual dream role of CEO.

When: David was attending an upcoming Top Leaders meeting, a leadership talent event which the CEO was hosting. This was the perfect opportunity. The CEO would be in a very benevolent state of mind at that event – in mentoring mode, and in appreciation of his organization's top talent – and so he would be more open and more nurturing versus being in impatient operational mode.

How: Ahead of the event, David asked for a thirty-minute one-to-one meeting during lunch to discuss the topic of 'shaping a better future in uncertain times'. During this meeting – when David had presented his innovative ideas, and felt confident that it was going well – he asked the CEO if he would consider David for Chief Strategy Officer the next time the role was vacant. He presented a three-year vision for the role and first-hundred-days priorities. After the meeting, David reached out to key influencers to ask them to support him as a candidate for the role.

Result: David was appointed Chief Strategy Officer within six months of asking the right person, at the right time, in the right way. The CEO needed an injection of fresh energy and intellect into that role, and David solved it for him by presenting himself.

The moral of the story is that when you commit, you make your own luck.

Be ready to learn, grow and change

You also need to put in the work to ensure role readiness for your promotion, by investing in your learning and development, staying up to date on hot topics, and addressing any skills gaps relevant to your desired promotion. If you have learned anything as you have been reading this book, it is probably that you will need to take risks and move outside your comfort zone if you want to secure the promotion you desire. You need to continue to grow and change if you want to continue to progress in your career. You can't be half in and half out if you want to secure your promotion; you need to commit and be all in. Each promotion is a step up, and ahead of the appointment decision you usually need to prove that you can do what it takes – so take responsibility for investing in your development, growth and change, both now and going forward. Demonstrate your willingness and capacity to learn and adapt. Show others that you have a keen desire to stretch yourself and fulfil your potential.

Here are some key 'learn, grow, change' building blocks that it will serve you well to incorporate and demonstrate in your current role and approach, as evidence of your future potential for a promotion role:

- Learning mindset

- Growth mindset

- Resilience

- Experience

- High energy

- High potential

- Strong work ethic

Learning mindset

Decision-makers want clever people on their teams. They seek out people who are fundamentally smart and open to continuous learning. You need to showcase examples that demonstrate you are able to learn new skills quickly, are willing and capable of processing new information, and have the intellectual capacity to reverse or make decisions based on new information.

Invest in your own learning and development by doing the following:

✓ Keep up to date with hot topics and your customers' areas of interest

✓ Find relevant industry conferences – ask if you can attend and represent the company

✓ If you need to improve your public-speaking skills, consider joining a debate club

✓ Consider privately hiring an executive coach/an independent truth-teller, who will work through feedback

you receive at work and help you to identify unhelpful
blind spots

✓ Be alert to what business schools have on offer as short
courses in executive education relevant to the role you
desire – or find your own service providers after work
or at the weekends

Growth mindset

Decision-makers want team members with a growth mindset:
people with the right attitude for an uncertain and unpredict-
able business world in which it is essential to keep growing
and learning and adapting to a constantly changing
environment.

A growth mindset is the opposite of a fixed mindset. With a
fixed mindset, people believe their basic qualities, like intelligence or talent, are fixed traits. They spend their time document-
ing their intelligence or talent, instead of developing it. They
also believe that talent alone creates success – without effort.
This is a type of stuck mindset that is self-limiting.

With a growth mindset, people believe that their core abilities can be developed through dedication and hard work – and
that brains and talent are just the starting point. These people
have a love of learning and a progressive attitude that is essential for great accomplishments.

Resilience

Resilience has probably become the most important currency
of today's disruption and uncertainty climate. It is the capacity
to recover quickly from tough challenges and sudden setbacks.
Decision-makers seek people who have demonstrated proof of
perseverance in life or work, and who can give examples of

having bounced back quickly from any failures and have shown an ability to modify their approach if the current one is not working. Demonstrate your ability to persevere when the going gets tough.

Experience

Decision-makers want to recruit people to their team who bring good judgement and the wisdom of experience, without any negative baggage such as a lack of drive to try new things or new ways of working. Experience brings a maturity and wisdom to the table, which is a huge value-add when it comes to spotting patterns in advance, not repeating previous mistakes, and making suggestions on how to anticipate and mitigate future issues.

High energy

Decision-makers want people who thrive on challenges, have something to prove and feel a relentless drive to succeed. Energy is about motivation, passion, commitment and ambition. Someone can be very experienced but lack the energy and drive for new challenges. Energy provides the necessary forward momentum to move through challenges and reach the desired end state.

High potential

The people who get promoted are those who have future capacity for development. Potential is about the latent qualities or abilities that may be developed and lead to future success. With the ever-accelerating pace of change in the marketplace, decision-makers are recognizing that the most important thing about employees is not where they come from (past achievements) but how far they can go (future potential).

Strong work ethic

You also need to demonstrate that you consistently work hard in your current role, and prove you have a strong work ethic. By 'work ethic', I mean that you are prepared to do what it takes to get your work done day to day: you solve problems, you put in longer hours when necessary, you are determined, you possess good self-discipline and are self-motivated, and you are resilient and resourceful when faced with a difficult challenge. These types of traits impress decision-makers, and will stand you in very good stead for future promotions.

Start behaving like a leader now

Eventually, all promotions result in a leadership position, so with the long game in mind, it would be strategic to start behaving like a leader now – even if you have no leadership title, no power base and no formal permission to lead yet. Remember, promotions are all about your future potential, so demonstrating early signs that you are a leader will give decision-makers more confidence in you.

You don't need to wait for permission or the 'right' role title to show your leadership capabilities. Anyone with the desire to lead can choose to do so. We need look no further than Greta Thunberg as an inspiring example of someone who had no leadership title or position of power. She went from being a schoolgirl on strike to being nominated for the Nobel Peace Prize, lecturing the UN and world leaders, and changing the world.

Leading from a low-power base

Take inspiration from Greta Thunberg as a contemporary role model who became a global leader despite starting out with no position of power in society, no role title and no formal authority or permission to lead. From a zero-power base, within a year Greta had brought her vision of a better and more sustainable future to the attention of world leaders.

Having started out as a lone schoolgirl on a lone strike, Greta is an example of how fast you can grow a leadership platform using only your personal power, being driven by your own values and speaking your truth. The world sat up and paid attention to Greta. Still only a teenager, Greta was nominated for the Nobel Peace Prize in 2019, named 'Person of the Year' by *Time* magazine that same year, and was invited to present her point of view to world leaders at the World Economic Forum in Davos in 2020.

Leadership is about having a vision or a big idea about how things could be in the future, persuading others to back you, and achieving great results. Whether you have a leadership post now or are yet to reach that goal, here are the ways you can start behaving like a leader:

- ✓ Talk about long-term future goals and not just immediate tasks

- ✓ Suggest a team away-day to discuss team strategy and mission

- ✓ Bring game-changing ideas to the next team meeting

✓ Be a good role model and try to inspire others

✓ Take more responsibility for leading other people or teams

✓ Offer to take on some of your boss's workload

✓ Bring the solution as well as the problem

✓ Ask your boss if you can take responsibility for specific projects

✓ Challenge constructively – and always with a positive attitude

✓ Be collaborative and create win–win scenarios

| Figure 4: Behaving like a leader

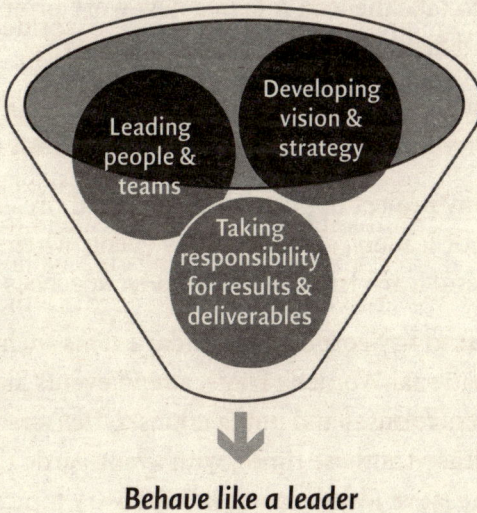

Behave like a leader

Don't wait for your organization to develop your leadership skills – take charge and make the effort to invest in yourself.

Company leadership development offerings typically lag behind actual role appointments – so you are only offered leadership-skills development *after* you secure a leadership role. By being proactive about developing your leadership skills ahead of any promotion, you are up-skilling yourself – putting yourself ahead of your peers and giving yourself a better shot at promotion. Be prepared to spend your own time and funds on developing yourself if necessary. See your career trajectory and promotion achievements as returns on that investment.

Here are some ideas on what you can do to gain more leadership experience in your current role:

✓ Volunteer to supervise or manage another person – maybe a new joiner – so that later you can show you have experience in managing someone else

✓ Offer to take the lead role in a new work project or be the lead facilitator at peer-level meetings

✓ Ask for stretch roles or special projects on the basis that they present leadership learning opportunities for you

✓ Take any project opportunities to gain more exposure to senior leaders, and attend any events where you can listen and learn from keynote leader speeches

✓ Be alert to key corporate calendar events such as International Women's Day – attend events and/or read the press releases and publications. Often special reports are released at these times, with avant-garde thinking and the latest ideas around key industry topics, and you may discover some great concepts that you could introduce into your organization

✓ Read business books and biographies, which are great for cutting-edge thinking and very inspiring. Stop by the bookshop when you're in the airport, and check the Top 20 business books to stay up to date on the hot topics. Biographies of successful individuals can also be very motivating; there are always lessons to be learned from the experiences of others

✓ Listen to leadership podcasts, TED Talks, webinars and audiobooks in your own time – perhaps on your commute to work

While you wait for your promotion, you could try to negotiate leadership development rewards from your boss in exchange for continued exceptional performance in your current role. Your boss may be able to allocate company budget towards your development. Perhaps you can persuade them to let you attend day or week courses during working hours, on the basis of a strong return on investment through your performance in your current role. There is also no shortage of material available online.

I highly recommend you try to find courses and events that will improve key aspects of leadership intelligence, such as emotional intelligence, digital intelligence and creative intelligence. Study areas that will challenge your thinking, and showcase your new leadership skills in your current role – don't wait for some undetermined future date to show how great you are now!

6   Confidence

Build your confidence

Stakeholders and decision-makers need to be confident that you can do the new job. They can look at the evidence of your track record and any number of other factors, but in the final analysis they are also taking a leap of faith that you are the right candidate for the role. It is never a sure bet, because you have not done this exact role before, with this exact team, in this exact economy. For reassurance, they will often take their lead from you.

If you are confident in your own abilities, others are more likely to back you. If you don't believe in yourself, it makes it more difficult for others to believe in you. Just to be crystal clear, taking steps to nurture your confidence is definitely not the same as 'fake it until you make it'. It is also worth stating that confidence and capability are linked but are not the same thing. You are probably very capable in your role, which is why you are now looking for a step-up role, but – as I continue to emphasize – capability alone will not get you the promotion.

When considering you for a promotion, decision-makers will look at your capability track record, your reputation, your passion for the role, your potential – and, though this may not be stated explicitly, they will take a view on whether you seem confident that you can handle the step-up challenge. No one knows what the future will bring in terms of challenges in a new role, or new team or new economy – but if you present yourself as someone who is confident that they can handle issues, stay calm and respond to challenges, then you are viewed as less of a risk in terms of the decision to appoint you.

Here are some great approaches to building and improving your confidence levels:

Appreciate what you have achieved

Take a moment to reflect on what you have achieved to date, and make a list of your accomplishments. Only you really know what it has taken for you to get this far – maybe it was long hours studying at school and university, or the courage needed during your first role and first year of work to keep turning up and learning about the world of work, or maybe you had significant personal setbacks in your journey that you had to overcome along the way. Connect with who you are and where you have come from, and appreciate how far you have travelled to reach your current level of success. Use this as a solid base of proof that you have specific skills, talent and work ethic – and rely on this as evidence to build your confidence so that you can go even further.

It is worth highlighting that you should also appreciate your efforts when situations did not go according to plan. You don't always have to come out on top to acknowledge that you tried your best. I am sure there are times when you tried and you didn't achieve your goals – but you learned from the experience.

Build your support base

Consider whether you feel supported – and if not, what steps you could take to build a more robust network of wise and encouraging people, including friends, family, mentors and advisors. A sense of belonging and feeling encouraged will boost your confidence levels, and keep you feeling secure during challenging times. No matter how strong we are, it is always helpful to be reassured and reminded by others that we have what it takes to get to the next level. Having people around us who believe in us and encourage us gives us the strength we sometimes lack.

Realize that it's okay to ask for help

Confident people are the first to ask others for help. They have the capacity to show their vulnerability, and are open to advice and learning. No one expects you to be superhuman. Not even the best leaders know everything – and certainly in this world of uncertainty and accelerated technological change, you can't possibly have all the answers all the time. A refusal to ask for help is so self-limiting, because it prevents you from solving the problem in front of you. An additional upside of having others help you is that you will all feel more bonded as you are working on ideas together, and you are more likely to help each other in the future as well.

Observe what triggers a confidence dip

Certain situations are well known to cause confidence dips. Being more aware of what is triggering the dips will enable you to manage them better, and help you to return more swiftly to normal confidence levels.

For example, if you have been rejected for a promotion in the past, thinking about trying again might cause a confidence dip. Don't let past rejection paralyse you and prevent you from moving forward. Rejection hurts, but it doesn't have to hold you back from trying again. Distance yourself from any previous rejection by practising self-compassion. Acknowledge your emotions if you felt embarrassed, sad, disappointed or discouraged. Deal with uncomfortable feelings head-on, because this is essential to coping with the discomfort in a healthy manner. Soothe yourself with the fact that it is natural to feel trepidation about trying again, but remind yourself that you are more experienced now and are better equipped to overcome any challenges.

Reframe mistakes and failures as growth opportunities

We all make mistakes. It is part of the human condition, and one of the key ways we learn and grow. In fact, mistakes are the necessary price you pay to learn a lesson and grow as a person – and the lesson and the growth are what you reap as the permanent dividend. So the upfront cost of the mistake results in a long-term repayment – and, as such, is well worth it!

Rather than criticizing or judging yourself when you make a mistake, accept what happened, learn the lesson and move on.

Reassure yourself: 'If other people can do it, so can I'

Look around you at the people at the next level up, and those who are even more senior. There is no need to be intimidated. I am pretty sure each of them has something impressive about them – but they are certainly not perfect. Whenever I thought about my next promotion, it seemed daunting at first. However, when I reflected on the flaws of those more senior than me (for example, someone who was extremely intelligent but had poor people-management skills) and my skills and potential in relation to my peers, it seemed less formidable. I had sufficient self-worth to know that I was as good as them, or had something fresh and unique to bring to the table. I remember thinking, 'If that person over there can do it, then so can I.'

One of my CEO clients told me a story he told himself when he first needed to push himself forward to the next level. When he was younger and learning to drive, it seemed so challenging, but he looked around him and saw all the other ordinary people like him who had mastered the ability to drive, and it reassured him that if all these people could do it, then so could he.

Sometimes it is comforting to know that – although it feels scary to try to achieve something new – other people have proved that it is possible, so take confidence from that, steel yourself and keep moving forward.

Tackle imposter syndrome

Imposter syndrome is a condition worth understanding in case you are affected by it. It is a negative thought process or psychological pattern in which a person doubts their accomplishments and has a persistent fear of being exposed as a 'fraud'. Sound familiar? Often, despite clear evidence that someone is great at their job, those experiencing imposter syndrome remain convinced that they are frauds and do not deserve all they have achieved. They put their success down to luck, or interpret it as a result of them deceiving others into thinking they are more intelligent than they themselves think they are.

Imposter syndrome is characterized by perfectionism and overachievement, and yet, in parallel, also a simultaneous undermining of one's own achievements, a fear of failure, and not being able to accept praise. It is a vicious cycle of overwork and overachievement: you never feel any better about the success, so you work even harder, achieving even more and still never feeling good. It is a feeling of inferiority inside you, and very often no one would imagine, from the outside, that you feel this way. Although you outwardly appear very accomplished, on the inside you think this success is accidental, some kind of favour or luck – and that one day soon you will be 'found out'. You don't think you deserve your success, and you don't think you have done anything to earn it.

Imposter syndrome is quite common in the corporate world – some might even go so far as to say that the corporate system enables it, so that employees are kept feeling insecure and continuously strive to achieve more and more.

Top tips for tackling imposter syndrome

Talk about it: A good way to tackle imposter syndrome is to talk to others and share how you feel. You may find out that they feel the same. It can be a relief to know that you are not alone, and it may alleviate a lot of the pressure you are putting yourself under.

Use logic, not emotion: Don't let your anxious feelings override the facts of the situation. Acknowledge what you bring to the table – it simply cannot be possible that you add no value at all. Identify your key strengths and what you are particularly good at. Appreciate what you have learned to date as being the sum of important experiences you now bring to any situation. Think about any patterns in positive feedback you receive at work – if everyone is observing the same positive attribute, it is quite likely to be actually true, so accept it. If your work culture is not a place for positive feedback, then go to friends or family to discuss your feelings and ask them to help you.

Memory-bank your successes: Commit your successes to memory. Remember the times when you were trying to achieve something and you faced significant adversity, and yet you came through and survived and learned from the experience. Realize that you have achieved so much, and try to stop giving yourself such a hard time by having to prove yourself again and again.

Calm your inner critic: Replace your harsh thoughts about yourself with what your kind best friend might say to you in this moment. You might be beating yourself up about not getting a promotion fast enough, and your best friend might say to you that it is better to be patient and figure out the role you really want, rather than be rushed into a more stressful situation for the sake of a faster promotion. Have compassion for yourself.

Imposter syndrome affects both men and women, though early research focused on the latter. Here is Michelle Obama talking about the issue in relation to women and girls in particular:

Imposter syndrome is so tough. For so long, women and girls have been told we don't belong in the classroom, boardroom, or any room where big decisions are being made. So when we do manage to get into the room, we are still second-guessing ourselves, unsure if we really deserve our seat at the table. We doubt our own judgment, our own abilities, and our own reasons for being where we are. Even when we know better, it can still lead to us playing it small and not standing in our full power.

I've been there plenty of times. What's helped me most is remembering that our worst critics are almost always ourselves. Women and girls are already up against so much: the fact is that you wouldn't be in that room if you didn't belong there. And while negative thoughts are bound to crop up as you take on new roles and challenges, you can acknowledge them without letting them stop you from occupying space and doing the work. That's really the only way we grow – by moving beyond our fears and developing trust that our voices and ideas are valuable.

Step outside your comfort zone

Everyone likes being in their comfort zone – that relaxed state in which things feel familiar and you are in control of your environment, and in which you experience low levels of anxiety and stress. In this zone, a steady level of performance is possible, but you will need to push yourself out of your comfort zone if you want to get promoted.

In my experience, people are capable of so much more than they think. We all enjoy being good at what we do – but unless we challenge ourselves and take more risks, we are in danger of becoming too complacent. Taking risks may seem scary at first, but the ultimate payoff is that moving out of your comfort zone will build your confidence levels and help you advance.

So what can you do to take yourself out of your comfort zone?

✓ Speak up

✓ Speak in public

✓ Learn a new skill

✓ Meet new people

✓ Take charge of a new project

✓ Volunteer, and embrace new challenges

✓ Try new experiences that slightly scare you

By definition, everything outside your comfort zone will be un-comfortable. When you feel challenged in this way, take a moment to reassure yourself that this is a positive sign that you're trying something new and different. When you are steeling yourself to move out of your comfort zone, ask yourself, 'What's the worst that could happen?' For example, when you ask for the promotion, you fear you might be rejected. If this happens, it's not the end of the world. You can choose to take it on the chin and learn from the experience – and try again another time, in another way.

Think about examples of when you have moved out of your comfort zone, and the positives that ensued. Look at others who have done it and take inspiration from them. Perhaps you should create stakes so high that not doing something is worse than staying safely in your comfort zone. Be driven by your sense of purpose and mission, and force yourself into taking risks.

I remember when I worked for a major consulting firm, I was too nervous to ask questions of senior leaders in open meeting forums, in case I said the wrong thing and people would judge me and find me lacking. I would feel frustrated with myself afterwards for not having more courage and not getting the answers to specific questions burning inside me. As a baby step, I would test out my questions on colleagues after the meeting, and their reaction gave me confidence that I could have spoken up. Eventually I forced myself out of my comfort zone – and started asking the questions in public. I realized that my questions were valid, and that getting answers from company leaders was appropriate and more important than my fear and discomfort. I started asking more sophisticated questions. Over time, it became enjoyable to challenge more senior people and assess if their answers were good enough. Now I work as a leadership advisor, and make a living out of fearlessly challenging leaders and asking very difficult questions! Pushing yourself to deliberately leave your comfort zone opens up new possibilities and accelerates your advancement.

A visualization exercise

It might be helpful to visualize your comfort zone as a small circle. Set your intention to master new challenges and expand into a bigger circle outside that small circle. Eventually it will become your new comfort zone, and then you can expand into another, bigger new circle, and so on – as in the diagram below. Once you see it more like a process, you will feel more comfortable doing it.

The words 'comfort' and 'confidence' are interchangeable in this instance. As you expand your comfort zone, you expand your confidence zone too.

| Figure 5: Expanding your comfort zone

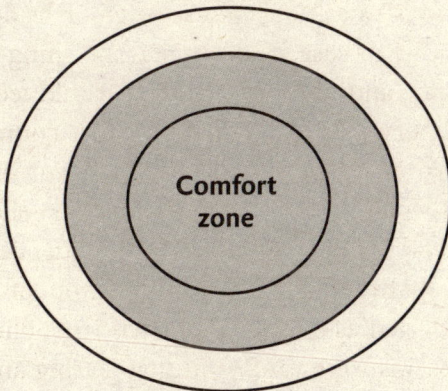

Circles are a helpful way of thinking about comfort zones because a new circle gives you the perception of having a new bounded area within which to operate – rather than feeling you are totally exposed and out of control if you step outside your current comfort zone. Reassure yourself that you don't have to push yourself too far too fast. It is about finding a balance – feeling almost too scared to reach for the next goal, but not letting that fear completely paralyse you and prevent you from moving forward.

Reframe your current comfort zone as your 'danger zone' – dangerous because it prevents you from improving, stops you from achieving all the things that you are capable of achieving, and eventually life becomes dull.

You bought this book because you are craving more, and have probably acknowledged that you feel you can do better. So you are now poised to move out of your comfort zone. You want tips and techniques to help you, but I also want you to be open to taking risks and forcing yourself out of your comfort zone. I can make lots of suggestions, but in the end you need to decide if you are going to push yourself to make it all happen.

7   Credibility

Stand out from your peers

When you want a promotion, you need to show great results in your current role, backed up by a great work ethic. You need to consistently meet your targets – and show great potential for the next level up. This is all fantastic for your promotion chances if you are the only standout candidate – but what happens when most of your peers within your team or across other teams are doing the same? If more candidates for the available promotion slots are performing at the same high standard, then this just means the bar is set even higher for promotion.

The way you can give yourself an edge over the competition is by already starting to operate at the next level up, proving that you have moved beyond 'potential'. This makes you a lower-risk option versus your peers. Becoming a credible candidate for promotion means you need to act at a more senior level of capability, professionalism and reliability – above what would normally be expected of someone in your current role. The most impactful way to do that is to start performing some of the functions of the next-level-up role – so much so that the promotion becomes the de facto admin stamp that you have already stepped up. The promotion lags behind the performance.

Many companies have a deliberate promotion strategy of

waiting for you to prove you can take on the next role before they award the promotion pay rise or title. This goes beyond showing your potential, and means you have actually already taken on the more senior responsibilities. Demonstrating evidence that you have taken on extra responsibilities creates pressure on your boss and decision-makers to move you forward and even fast-track you in your career. For example, if your next move is to manage a team of people, and you have already shown people-management skills by successfully leading a small group project initiative, then this is evidence that your skills are in play already.

How to show you are promotion-ready

✓ Demonstrate an ongoing drive to improve yourself

✓ Show a willingness to take on extra responsibilities

✓ Show maturity when dealing with setbacks or failure

✓ Display a talent for leadership

✓ Respond constructively to feedback

✓ Be self-directed and take the initiative

✓ Enlist your colleagues to support your promotion

How to show you understand the transition risk

You can also differentiate yourself from your peers by displaying a greater understanding of any transition risk inherent in moving up to the next major role. When you can align yourself with how the decision-maker thinks, they will rate you even more highly as a credible standout candidate. The decision-maker may have put a question mark over how candidates will cope with the step-up transition. All other things being equal in the mind of the decision-maker, they will opt for the less risky candidate.

For example, you may be a successful leader of 25 people in one country, and your next promotion role is to manage 250 people across Europe. You may have 'proven' people-management skills, but in your current job you can reach out to everyone within your direct report team very quickly and easily, and can be personally responsive to your people when required. Not so in the new role – you would need to find a way to change your communications approach so you can inspire and engage more people with less direct access. You would also have different geographical and cultural challenges – ranging from simple time differences when scheduling meetings to more complex issues around cultural norms and style preferences. Another candidate for the same promotion, who has proven people-management skills and has already made a successful transition to a country abroad, will have an edge on you. In this specific case, a mitigating point in your favour would be if you had successfully led a cross-cultural team. Demonstrating your awareness and understanding of the risk makes the decision-maker feel more confident about you.

Key major role transitions include:

- Moving from being an individual contributor to managing others

- Moving from managing a small team to managing a significantly larger group

- Moving from functional head to a general manager

- Moving from local responsibility to national or global responsibility

- Moving from mature markets to emerging markets experience (and vice versa)

- Moving to a new company after a significant length of time at a previous company

These types of transitions cannot be underestimated. For example, if you have worked for ten years in your current company and are changing company for the first time, there will be an inherent transition risk in moving to a new company culture – where you cannot simply get things done by virtue of knowing the right people and knowing how things work in this environment. Moving to a new company means a total reset of your cultural understanding and your reservoir of relationship goodwill – and it can be extremely challenging. So the decision-maker may be minded to choose an internal candidate who does not pose that same risk. But perhaps the decision-maker can be persuaded to choose you if you explain that you have made several moves within your current company which could be regarded as similar resets.

If your desired promotion involves a major transition, who-ever has the decision to promote you will need to be confident not just that you can do the new role when everything has settled down, but that you can actually cope with the initial transition challenges involved. The decision-maker is placing an investment bet on you.

Try to see the risks from the decision-maker's point of view, and try to demonstrate a track record of difficult transitions that you successfully coped with in the past. Ideally, you will show past experiences that mirror the transition challenges ahead, for example previous promotion transition successes, any experience where you moved geographically, or maybe that special project where you reported to a manager in a different country or had to work as part of a cross-cultural team. It will comfort the decision-maker if you are ready to acknowledge that the transition will be challenging – rather than simply saying it won't be a problem. It may give you the edge over other candidates. Decision-makers will be more confident in you if they feel you are self-aware, mature, and realistic about what is ahead. Together, you can figure out a support system or any initial compensating mechanisms you might need – such as a company mentor or executive coach for the first twelve months of the transition.

Build a strong reputation

Your reputation is a widespread belief held by others about the characteristics you possess. How others perceive you is so important when it comes to a decision about whether you are ready for a step-up promotion. While you cannot totally control the conclusions other people come to, it should be reassuring to know that you have the most determining influence on what they perceive. Reputation is not something that just happens in a void, nor is it something you should leave to chance. You control what you do, what you say, how you behave.

Do you want to know the secret to building a good reputation? Become a person who deserves one! Consistency is the key, so with a promotion in mind, try to build up a strong track record of doing what you said you would do: delivering results on time and within budget; being known to have good ideas and following through on them to add value.

| Figure 6: Your reputation hierarchy

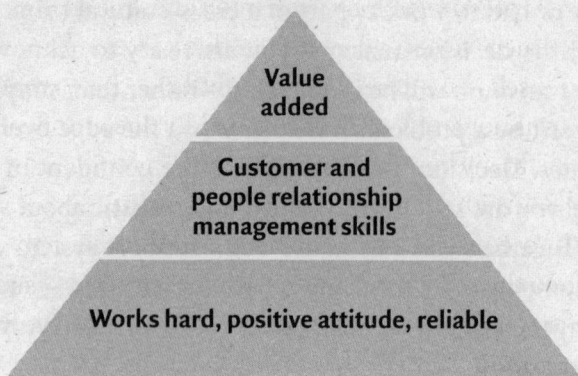

Value added

Customer and people relationship management skills

Works hard, positive attitude, reliable

This diagram can be useful when prioritizing the characteristics that you would like to highlight at different stages of your career. Those on the first layer – work ethic, reliability and a positive attitude – are entry-level characteristics. They are your bread and butter. You'll need to present all of these characteristics to move on from an entry- or junior-level position to the next stage.

The middle layer means demonstrating more responsibility and an ability to manage people – in short, great interpersonal skills. Organizations are highly interpersonal places, so making a great impression on your customers, colleagues and your manager is key. Getting a reputation for being likeable and easy to work with is important – because people will be open to working with you, and will be more likely to help you when you need a problem solved or when you need an extra pair of hands.

Finally, the top layer is your ability to add value above and beyond what is expected in your role or at your level. This is about those specific skill areas where you are rated in your current role appraisals with the equivalent of an 'exceeds expectations'. If you want to get promoted, you have to exceed expectations in at least some aspects of your current role, so that there is pressure to move you into a more challenging one.

To become a value-adder, start to think like one. Do this by asking yourself – like a daily mantra, until it becomes embedded in your consciousness – 'How can I add value at this meeting when I talk to my boss . . . when I am with my team . . . with my customers?' With a value-add mindset, you are always seeking out ways to constructively contribute to the moment, to the meeting, to the milestone, to improving performance . . . It becomes a way of being which others will notice and appreciate.

Play to your key strengths to ensure that you are seen as adding value at meetings, beyond your role, to the wider organization and even your industry. For example, you could develop a specialist expertise in a particular area, and advise others, speak at events and post articles on this topic – thus building up a reputation as the person to consult if an issue within this area ever comes up. Think about your natural talents and strengths, and then play to these strengths to differentiate yourself. Oftentimes we undervalue what we are good at – when something comes easily to us, we may wrongly assume it comes easily to other people too. So the first step is to look back at your performance appraisals and think about which areas of your work or behaviour you receive consistent praise about. These are signals to you about how others rate you.

Consider the following questions:

- What are your key strengths?

- What is unique about you?

- What talent or experience sets you apart from your peers and teammates?

Your strength could be that you are an all-round capable person – i.e. your consistency, your reliability, being known as a 'safe pair of hands' day to day or in a crisis. These are good qualities, but they may keep you stuck in middle management. To break free of the middle, what works better is becoming known for a unique talent, for example as 'an incredible deal-maker' or 'totally customer-centric' or 'very decisive' or 'the smartest person in the room' or 'very insightful'. What specific strengths and talents could you hone into a brand reputation strapline about what is different about you?

Shore up your reputation by finding new ways to impress and stand out from your peers – such as landing a new key client account, or closing a significant and financially lucrative deal, or winning an award for your team for great customer service. Pay close attention to any customer feedback, both positive and negative – and find ideas for improving customer relations or new product and service opportunities. Think about what process areas are not working or are broken, and what you can do to fix them. Be aware of what is going on in your company and sector as a whole. Follow your CEO on social media to understand their agenda, and try to align your ideas accordingly. Read the latest material on thought leadership and/or attend conferences to hear about trends in your industry.

Gaining a great reputation is not an overnight transactional event – instead it is a process built up over time and with increasing experience. When you are making an impact, don't be shy about sharing what you are working on and telling people about your successes. Don't hide your light under a bushel; publicize your results. Try to work on high-profile projects so that senior decision-makers notice you. Your reputation has to be earned – it is not something that automatically comes with a role promotion. In fact, it is the other way around – you will get the promotion once you have built up a great reputation and earned the trust of others and their confidence that you can lead at the next level up.

Your relationship with your boss is critical to building and sustaining a strong reputation. Your boss is very well placed to add or detract from your overall credibility, because this person sees how you behave under pressure. Other people know this and will be very inclined to believe what your boss says about you. You need to try to get along with your boss as much as you try to get along with your teammates. Even if you don't highly rate everything about your boss, think of them as someone you can learn from and someone who you need to get onside if you want to build up a good reputation at their peer level. The term 'managing upwards' is often used in corporate organizations – it refers to your ability to manage your boss and other senior folks. Try to manage a great upwards relationship with your boss, where they are impressed with your ability in your current role and also supportive of your ambitions for promotion.

Be trustworthy

Alongside strategies on how to build a positive reputation and enhance your credibility for promotion is an equally important list of how you can lose credibility fast. This is what *not* to do if you want to be trustworthy and impress your stakeholders. It is worth 'naming and shaming' these behaviours in case any of them ring true and you didn't realize that they are getting in the way of your promotion.

✘ *Failing to follow through when you promise to do something*

When you commit to delivering a key change or completing a task and you don't deliver, then how can anyone trust you the next time you agree to do anything? Even when you try to mitigate a lack of follow-through with a plausible explanation, you will still lose some credibility. When you agree to take on the responsibility for completing a task, make sure you can deliver on it before you promise to do it. Don't take the short-term gain of pleasing others by putting up your hand at the meeting and volunteering, if in reality you know you cannot deliver. At the same time, don't be overly cautious to the point of never volunteering to lead anything. Choose tasks that you are realistically likely to succeed at, and have confidence in yourself that you are resourceful and will find a way through.

✘ *Not hitting your critical business targets*

If you can't be relied on to hit your targets in your current role, why would anyone put their faith in you that you can deliver in a more pressurized role? Consistency is the key. Of course there will be quarters or years when missing your key business targets is more of a macro issue, such as when the company sets overly ambitious targets or if there is a sudden economic downturn in your industry or the economy. You are only human, so you can't be 100 per cent consistent.

✘ *Not managing expectations*

There is only one thing more serious than missing a critical business target or deadline, and that is when it is not signalled in advance to your key stakeholders. In business, no one likes surprises. Always set expectations in advance if you are unlikely to hit your target or deadline. Don't wait until the last moment to let people know, as then it may be too late for others to help you or create compensating plans.

✖ *Not being loyal to your boss or company brand*

It is good to challenge your boss constructively, but don't deliberately embarrass your boss or any senior stakeholder by challenging them aggressively in front of others. If you feel strongly about an issue or have a key area of concern, then try to resolve it one-to-one. If you want to become more senior, your boss and their peers need to be assured that they can trust you with confidential information. You may be made privy to details about future restructuring or redundancy plans, and you need to be trusted with that sensitive information. You will lose credibility fast if senior management realize that you gossip behind your boss's back, or have no loyalty to the company that is paying your wages.

✖ *Acting unethically, covering your tracks, telling lies*

You might think that acting unethically is an obvious no-no and that this goes without saying. But it is worth mentioning that – alongside the big unethical acts like corporate fraud which you would never consider – there are small, everyday unethical acts like lying. You may see this as just a harmless habit and not realize how one small lie can lead to a major lack of trust in you. Don't ever lie about anything – big or small. Don't try to cover your tracks if you do something wrong. We all make mistakes. Just be upfront when you make yours. It is more impressive when your colleagues know that you always tell the truth and are capable of owning up to an honest mistake. They will be more confident in you when they can trust you to tell them what is going on, even when it makes you look bad in the short term.

✘ *Complaining, making excuses, creating drama*

The saying 'a bad workman blames his tools' always rings true when I hear people blaming anything and everyone for why they couldn't do their work properly. If you are having work problems, you need to problem-solve – not just complain about it or put the blame everywhere else except yourself. Some people constantly create a dramatic performance out of everyday work activities, instead of calmly getting on with their tasks. Some make a huge amount of noise that is disproportionate to their contribution; they are noisy when they are complaining, noisy about how great they are when they do something well, noisy about everything and anything – so much so that, in the end, no one is listening to anything they say. These attention-seekers are actually self-sabotaging their chances of getting promoted, because by the time they finally do something impressive, everyone is drained and exhausted from all the noise and has lost interest in their antics.

✘ *Not staying up to date on tech and industry trends*

If you want to get promoted to the next level up, you can't be the last to know about the latest ideas or trends in your industry or area of work. You need to be ahead of the curve, the one bringing fresh ideas into the organization – not a laggard. Being a tech 'dinosaur' is a surefire way to lose credibility in today's high-tech, fast-paced world. So let's test you out on this right now: we all know that AI is becoming increasingly important in business, so what do you know about this topic and what it means for your business products and services? If you can't begin to answer this question, then you are already behind where you should be. Try to get ahead of new technologies and innovations and read up on new trends – and bring these topics into your workplace to see what changes you can initiate or influence. Become known as a cutting-edge thinker, not someone who is out of date and constantly having to catch up.

✗ *Taking credit for the work of others, not being a team player*
People who are not team players show little or no interest in the activities of the team, and rely on others to make decisions and carry out the real work. They fail to listen to teammates and do not seek to contribute to the welfare of the group. If you are only out for number one, you lose credibility with others because you are not able to collaborate. Organizations are made up of teams, and you have to find a way to be a team player if you want to survive in the system. Although your promotion is your singular goal for yourself, you should not act in a selfish way to achieve it. It is a big no-no to take credit for work outputs without thanking those who helped you to achieve your goals. It is more mature to show yourself as someone who has the grace to include others in your success, and people are more likely to want to help you going forward too.

You can build a great reputation and maintain credibility for promotion by setting high standards for yourself and living out those standards day to day. Take it from me that those around you will notice your improved professionalism – they will especially notice how you behave under pressure. Accept responsibility for your successes and failures. Always tell the truth. Keep your word. Always do your best. When people trust in you, and believe in you, their faith in you will grow and they will be happy to help you to progress in your career ambitions.

8   Campaign

Understand politics and culture

As mentioned previously, we all like to believe that we work in a meritocratic organization, and that promotion decisions are based solely on performance. The reality is that this is not the case – or at least, this is not the case all the time, and especially the more senior you become. At junior levels, more promotion opportunities are available, it is easier to differentiate one candidate from another, and the stakes are not that high for the decision-maker in terms of who gets promoted. But as you climb further up the company hierarchy and become more senior, there are fewer available roles – and investing in your promotion becomes more and more risky for the decision-maker because more power is centralized in each promotion role. There may also be political consequences for the decision-maker if they do not get it right.

At senior levels, internal politics play a larger role in the decisions that are made – and who does or doesn't get promoted will be affected by factors other than performance, including a history of power pacts and the currency of favours. Unwritten rules emerge, such as 'If you do me a favour now, I'll reward you with a favour later' or 'If you put my guy in now, I'll make your life easier'. Those at the very top levels are often insecure, so they are keen to have team members who are loyal supporters and will feed them information. They want people who can be relied upon not to topple them from their seat of power. Rewards like promotions are bestowed with the expectation of loyalty in return.

In some organizations this type of behaviour runs unchecked, but even if it doesn't in your company, don't be fooled into thinking your organization is totally free of politics. Where there are people, there are politics.

So many people get uncomfortable as soon as I bring up the word 'politics', and they immediately say 'I don't do politics' or 'I don't want to get involved in politics'. But it is important to learn about politics, as most people that decide to check out of the game stay stuck where they are. Rather than seeing politics as a bad practice, just see it as a human practice – something that happens when humans get together – and understand that political skill is simply a new leadership skill that you have to learn if you want to get ahead. Accept that politics play a part in determining who gets promoted, and decide that you are going to figure out the politics of your promotion. It is possible to be politically skilled enough to position yourself for promotion success, without compromising your integrity.

Engaging in politics is part of the overall method of delivering great results. You need to be alert to the norms and behaviour in your workplace culture, avoid any landmines, and align yourself with the people who have power and influence. You also need to be prepared to self-advocate.

Self-advocacy is about self-promotion, standing up for yourself, and being prepared to let the people in power know who you are, what you stand for, and why you deserve the promotion and their backing. Become more politically astute by taking the time to look past your day-to-day role, and notice what is going on around you in terms of political allegiances and power relationships among your colleagues, peers, bosses and more senior leaders. Start by noticing who holds the power in your organization, and think about the unwritten code of who, and what, really matters in your work culture. The people with the power are the people you need to network and build relationships with.

Look at those who have been promoted in the past and think about the following:

- What are the unwritten rules of promotion in your company?

- Who is getting promoted in your organization? And why?

- Who do they have relationships with? How did they achieve this?

- What types of behaviour are rewarded in this organization?

- What types of behaviour are not rewarded?

- Who seems to be in favour and why?

You can't just come to work and do your job and ignore the bigger picture. If you do, you will likely be blindsided at promotion time when 'out of nowhere' a less capable colleague is 'suddenly' promoted ahead of you, and you cannot comprehend how it happened. Trust me – it happened because you were not paying attention, because you were not alert to the politics around your promotion. You need to figure out who is in your corner already, and who else you need to build strong relationships with.

Also be aware that there are typically macro organization politics at play as different divisions grapple for power. It may be that you are doing a great job and are super ambitious with loads of potential, but there are negative inbuilt perceptions in your culture about your function or division. For example, people who work at company HQ who seek role promotions in the business units may find that there is an already-entrenched prejudice or disregard for perceived 'ivory tower' thinkers.

Notice what is happening below the surface of seemingly ordinary relationships around you. The following diagram illustrates some tactics you can deploy yourself if you want to be more politically astute:

| Figure 7: Be more politically astute

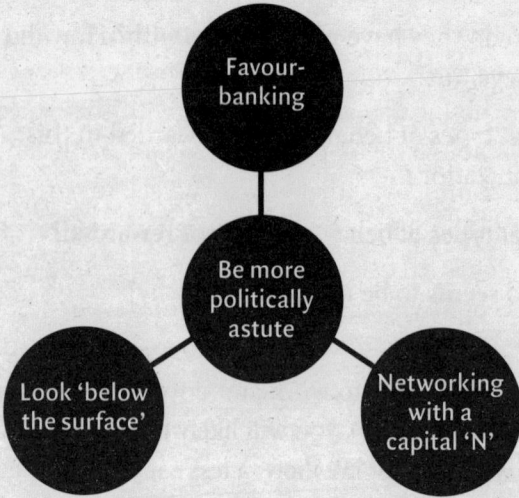

Favour-banking

When you are trying to accomplish your goals, first think about how you can help the other person. See it like a favour 'bank' where you make deposits and withdrawals. What favours can you do for someone that will mean they'll think more favourably about you? Also, there is an unwritten code or understanding that they will pay you back the favour at a later date. Ideally, you want your favour bank to be in credit all the time, so that most people owe you back a favour which you can call in when you really need it. The currency of favours is not as exacting as monetary value – but it seems to find its own level. For example, you might help someone out during a project crisis or team rebellion, and it may be left unsaid that they in turn will put in a positive word about you in their formal performance appraisal or during your promotion decision.

Some people, of course, are all take and no give, so if you realize that some people are not returning favours, you could ask outright for their support when you need it – the alternative is that everyone withdraws from helping each other, and this is a more negative outcome for everybody. Try not to be too calculating about depositing favours with the expectation of returns. Although the concept of a favour bank can be in the back of your mind – so that you are an active participant – try to be relaxed about it, or you spoil the effect. Just focus on being helpful and getting along with other people; and as night follows day, people will start returning some favours. Be easy with it and let it flow: you do favours for people, people do favours for you; sometimes you pay it forward and don't expect a specific return, sometimes people do something for you without expecting a return. It's all good.

Networking with a capital 'N'

You might dread the term 'networking', as it is often associated with making ridiculous small talk at semi-formal gatherings, and everyone handing out printed business cards. Often everyone is selling to everyone else, but nobody is in a position to buy. I call this 'networking with a small "n"', and it is largely pointless and a waste of everybody's time.

For some reason, people think networking just for the sake of networking is the goal itself, rather than being more purposeful. If you decide to network at an event, ask yourself who you really want to target and build a relationship with, and why. Otherwise you are leaving the whole thing up to chance, and you are unlikely to find yourself being introduced to the most important person in the room. Trust me – they have already been cornered by those who attended with real purpose.

Think about a person or a few key people you want to build a relationship with, maybe because they are in a position to mentor you or oil the wheels when you are seeking a promotion. Consider where you are most likely to meet them, and if it is at informal work events, then go along and network. This is networking with a capital 'N' – it is purposeful and outcome-oriented. In addition to targeting specific people, you could have a broader networking aim – to meet people from other parts of the organization or headquarters who could further fill you in on the bigger picture and where promotion opportunities might lie, now or in the future. You may find out more new information about opportunities from colleagues at social events than you would at official meetings – as long as they know you or feel they can trust you.

Look 'below the surface'

Switch on a radar in your head so you are attuned not just to what is being said in an explicit fashion – i.e. 'above the surface' – but what is also being left unsaid ('below the surface'). When you find yourself blindsided or confused by other people's behaviour or decisions, seek to look below the surface to uncover what is really going on. For every action or decision taken or behaviour displayed – rightly or wrongly – there is usually a very good reason; and just because you don't understand it, doesn't mean it doesn't exist.

You should practise seeking to understand what is happening below the surface by looking at underlying motivations, the strength of the relationships of the people involved, and who said what to whom and why – and then learn to astutely draw your own conclusions about what really happened and why. If possible, sense-check your conclusions with others; over time, you will grow your own ability to intuit why others behave the way they do. You could also do a course on organization politics and human behaviour, if you ever have the time!

Build influence and momentum

Armed with a better understanding of how politics can be your friend, let's think about how else you can build influence and create a groundswell of goodwill and support for your promotion.

Getting support for your promotion should never be left to the week or day before a vacancy comes up. Think of it as a long-term campaign that you need to plan for and work on throughout the year, in order to build up the right momentum in time for the promotion decision.

Invest the time to ensure you do the following:

✓ Stay visible throughout the year

✓ Sustain your impact

✓ Innovate

✓ Get your customers onside

✓ Repair any conflicts

✓ Get to know the CEO and senior leaders

✓ Get to know your boss's boss

✓ Handle the competition

Stay visible throughout the year

Raise your profile in your organization so that decision-makers and key influencers know who you are. Look out for opportunities to participate in high-profile projects sponsored by very senior leaders. Take any opportunity to introduce yourself to the key decision-makers and influencers during such projects – through your contributions or during the coffee breaks. You can also make yourself visible to them at company networking events, or by inviting them to meet your key customers, or by extending an invitation to hear a presentation by you and your team on the interesting work you're doing.

Whatever it takes – and you may have to go way outside your comfort zone – you have to be seen and become known by the people who are in a position to make decisions about or influence your career future. It may even mean having the courage to walk up to their office door and knock, just to say hello.

If the key people do not know you, and you have not made an effort to introduce yourself to them, why would they think you have the necessary initiative to undertake the role at the next level up?

Sustain your impact

It is not just decision-makers that need to be able to put a face to your name. It is beneficial to have good visibility and a high profile with as many people as possible within your company. In addition to your day-to-day work, think about what company-wide initiative you could lead or get involved in – this will raise your profile with more senior people across the organization. Pick something that has an appropriate context for you or is a cause you passionately believe in. For example, if you feel strongly about the role your company could play in combatting climate change, you could get involved in corporate environmental improvements.

The more passionate you are about a project, the more authentic your energy and participation will be. It will also help you feel motivated and fulfilled at work if you set up or participate in a cause that resonates with you. As your project gains support, you will feel more connected to your company purpose, and this will help you bring more positive energy to the workplace – and other people will notice your positive attitude and contributions.

Innovate

A great way to get noticed and be considered as a leader of the future is to be the person who brings a fresh idea to the table and persuades others that it is a good concept, gets funding for it and executes the project successfully. Aim to be seen as an innovator – someone with one foot in the future, who is in tune with current trends and can anticipate future products and services.

Put forward your ideas on what your team or company could be working on which would strengthen market positioning. Don't hold back if you don't (yet) see yourself as an 'ideas person'. Liberate yourself from such labelling. Ideas don't belong to a certain type of person; anyone can come up with great ideas. The path to innovation is just about being more curious and more confident – and questioning your work process and the bigger picture.

When approaching your work tasks, get into the habit of asking yourself: Is there a better way of doing this? How will this make a difference to the strategic outcome we are trying to achieve? Could we get to the end goal faster, or produce a more high-quality product, or be more efficient?

Get your customers onside

It is usually worth taking a risk and disclosing to your customers that your ambition is to get promoted this year. If you are doing a good job, they may be only too happy to become involved and put in a good word for you. Showing your vulnerability might strengthen the relationship too, as they may empathize with you because of something similar they have either already been through in their organization or are also going through now. Your success and your customers' success are inextricably intertwined. When you do a great job for your customer, they will get promoted – and because you will be seen as being part of their success, that in turn means they will be pleased to support *your* success.

I suppose there is a slight risk that disclosing your promotion ambitions to customers means they might use it as a bargaining chip and take advantage of you, but on balance I think it is worth taking that risk.

Repair any conflicts

It is better for you not to have any lingering arguments with colleagues or people in central functions like HR or finance, or any key individuals who you may have had a run-in with in the past. If you have conflicts that remain unresolved, such people may try to block your promotion – and succeed – because they have a grievance about that time you challenged them on budget permissions or holiday pay or whatever slight they felt you were responsible for. Some people are only too happy to wield what small power they have – dressed up in their firm belief that you were out of order and need to be put back in your place.

Part of the 'karma' of your organizational life is that old arguments left unresolved can come back to haunt you at exactly the wrong time. So take a moment now to think about who dislikes you, who seems to have taken against you, and whether you can do anything to recover that situation. In my experience, misunderstandings and resentments are usually easily cleared up by talking to the person about it, or complimenting their work, rather than ignoring the problem and thinking it will go away all by itself. Not everyone is going to like you all the time – and you can't control that. However, where you can repair a rift, then it is definitely in your self-interest to be the bigger person and heal it now.

Get to know the CEO and senior leaders

Read CEO and senior leadership communications. Follow the CEO on their social media channels to understand their strategic agenda and the kind of character they are. Don't be afraid to introduce yourself to the CEO when the opportunity arises. It is always good to have an elevator pitch ready – one or two lines on what you would say if you were stuck in an elevator with them. (I am not kidding, this actually happened one time to me when a client's CEO came into the elevator. Unfortunately I froze instead of taking advantage of the moment and creating a really positive connection.) Your 'elevator pitch' can simply be your name, your division, the name of your boss (which the CEO may recognize), a compliment, and a key headline regarding your work mission: 'Hello, I'm Fiona. I liked your Twitter comment on the important role big businesses can play on responding to climate change. Actually, I lead the environmental response initiative for our team in Dave Rawlinson's group.' One thing is for sure – CEOs love compliments. They will respond to say 'Thank you' and you can reply with something like 'Perhaps I could show you our work on this. I think you would find it interesting. Could I ask your PA to put a time in your diary?' CEOs are very confident people and they love other confident people. They will be impressed by your initiative.

Don't be nervous about getting to know your CEO or other senior leaders – they are people too. Just feeling that sense of connection with the senior leadership team, and being around them, might give you more confidence and spur you on to be a more inspiring senior leader yourself.

Get to know your boss's boss

This is of course related to the last point, but I want to advise you very specifically not to be afraid to build a relationship with your boss's boss. Your boss may be insecure and prefer to be the only one with a direct line of communication to their boss. They may have signalled this to you. However, this kind of hierarchical attitude is controlling and rigid. To be fair, your boss may just be blindly repeating a fear-based pattern they learned when they were in your position, which is 'never go over your boss'. In fact, you live and work in a democracy, and you should feel perfectly confident building a working relationship with anyone in the organization – including your boss's boss.

This doesn't mean that you are going over your boss's head or being disloyal – it just means having a chat or a line of communication to their boss about who you are, what you do and your progress. I see it as a show of confidence, and it may serve you well in the future if you have a difficult boss who tries to limit your progression, because then at least someone else senior has some knowledge of your potential and capability. Your boss may not like the new, more confident you talking to their own boss, so you should always avoid tension by applying the rule of never making your boss look bad – in fact, it could be a great opportunity to praise your boss, make them look good in front of their boss, and ensure everyone is happy!

Handle the competition

I am realistic about human behaviour, and I know that sometimes we are limited in our self-confidence and creativity. We might think that all this advice sounds difficult to execute and that really the best way to win the race for a promotion is to scupper the competition by spreading rumours or negative stories about them. But trust me – tearing down your competition so that you are the only man or woman left standing is not going to help you in the longer term. It is a negative way of securing your promotion, and it will backfire at some point. People have long memories, and if you played a dirty-tricks campaign against them, they are unlikely to go quietly. They might reveal your antics for all the world to see, and if that is not possible then they will likely wait in the long grass and plot their revenge. The best path to take is to invest all your energy and focus on winning by fair means rather than foul.

Of course, even when you hold yourself to a high standard, it won't stop other people from campaigning by spreading rumours or negative stories about you – especially if you are seen as a real threat to their advancement. Your competition may be clever enough to find your Achilles heel – or, ironically, an area of exceptional accomplishment – and weaponize it against you. I have seen this time and again, so I want to equip you with how to respond effectively.

First, try to strike the right balance between not being naive and not being paranoid about what your competition is doing in terms of negative campaigning against you. Second, stand up for yourself when untruths are being told about you. Do this robustly but without sounding defensive. It is more effective to politely assert yourself by directly asking your naysayer why they said something negative about you, than it is to ignore the situation. It is always good to address issues as a way of firing a warning shot – to let them know that no one is allowed to walk all over you. They may back down in the face of a show of strength, and might be disarmed by your directness and not want to upset you further.

If your detractors are clever, they will find a real weakness in you; and they will exploit it by shining a spotlight on it. For example, you might wait too long to make decisions, and this could be turned into 'He's too cautious – not the kind of person you want at your side during tough times and when tough decisions need to be made.' In those kinds of situations where a neutral or a negative is magnified, you need to own it – you need to say, 'Yes, I tend to wait for the right information before I make a decision, so that I am guided by the data and don't regret making the wrong decision later. However, I am prepared to adjust my style as and when the situation requires it.' Or say, 'Yes, this is true, but I am aware of it and it is something I am working on,' and give an example of what you are doing to change it.

When your star shines too bright for other people

All my advice is geared towards you empowering yourself, raising your profile and being successful. Your subsequent fast ascent may be too much for your competition to handle. I have seen a case where a client wrote a thought leadership book for the benefit of her company and clients, and also as a way to raise her profile. Her mistake was to be too explicitly self-praising in the book, which gave her jealous competition the ammunition to say that her motives were self-serving. The whole situation was made quite political, and the success of the book was actually weaponized against her.

When your star is shining bright, the light can be too bright for others. My best advice is to try to raise your profile without being too obviously self-promoting, so that others cannot turn your success against you. Change your intentions so that you are seeking your promotion for the benefit of everyone – your team, your customers, your organization – and not just yourself.

Pitch your First 100 Days plan

It is not enough to talk about what you have done in the past, or what you could do in the future in a theoretical sense. Try to ground your pitch in the form of a written plan of what you would seek to achieve by the end of your first 100 days in the new role. It is a great way to prove how you would tackle the role – without even being asked yet.

I recommend that, as soon as you have established the promotion opportunity you desire, start to draft your First 100 Days plan. Having to write the plan out forces you to really think about the role and how you would add value as the role-holder – and immediately you might identify information you need to gather, stakeholders you need to talk to, topics you need to research, and any missing skills or experience gaps that you need to fill. The early challenge of trying to write the role plan will test your commitment, and might also shock you into understanding the true gap between where you are now and where you need to be if you want to be considered as a serious candidate for the promotion. This awakening of self-awareness is only for your benefit. Embrace it, and take the steps necessary over the next few weeks or months to prepare.

During formal recruitment interviews for manager vacancies all the way up to CEO vacancies, it has become quite standard for the interview panel to ask candidates for their First 100 Days plan – i.e. what they would do in the first 100 days if they got the job. It gives the panel an opportunity to see how much the candidate has thought about how they would kick-start their performance in the new role. To be frank, it also allows the interviewers to gather the best ideas from all the candidates, which they then share with the successful candidate to further strengthen their original plan.

So whether you are crafting your next promotion as an entirely new role for the organization, or taking part in a formal process for an actual vacancy, you should always write up a First 100 Days plan for the new role as part of your own get-promoted project, regardless of whether you have been asked for one or not. When the plan is in great shape, send it to the key decision-maker as part of your get-promoted campaign, to impress upon them how much you want this role and why you would be the best choice.

To write your First 100 Days plan, start with the end in mind. Look ahead to what you would want to achieve by the end of three years in the role, and then list what your key priorities would be in the first twelve months. With that vision and context in mind, write down the list of the most important outcomes to be achieved by the end of your first 100 days. This approach is what will elevate your First 100 Days plan from a to-do list or set of themes to a more visionary, strategic big-picture document that will make the maximum impact.

Use the following structure to guide you.[1]

Your First 100 Days plan template

	Role aspirations by end of 3 years	Strategic priorities in first 12 months	Key desired outcomes by end of first 100 days
On Vision & Strategy			
On People & Teams			
On Results & Deliverables			

Across the three overarching categories of Vision & Strategy, People & Teams and Results & Deliverables, try to come up with between seven and ten key desired outcomes to be achieved by the end of your first 100 days. For example, under People & Teams, by the end of the first 100 days you may want to have assessed team capability versus the three-year role aspiration, made some key appointments, and launched a recruitment search for new talent.

Writing your plan on the basis of up to ten key outcomes shows that you are a person of action, not just ideas – and that

1 For more details, please refer to my book *Your First 100 Days: How to make maximum impact in your new leadership role* (2019).

you are focused on what you can get done. Decision-makers love a person with a plan, who knows what they want to achieve. It gives them a huge confidence uplift and reduces concerns about transition risk.

Use this plan as an opportunity to demonstrate your understanding of the key role issues and challenges, and why you are best placed to solve them. This is your chance to showcase your skills – and your true passion for the role. The decision-maker will be so impressed that you are determined in your pitch, and your plan can be used to kick-start discussions between you and them on what else needs to be done – and as such, you will already have started working together on the issues, and you become a more likely candidate in their eyes. The First 100 Days plan approach is a smart way to pitch with substance, and it will help you stand out from the competition.

9 Close

Negotiate and close the deal

The ideal scenario is that when you are offered the promotion role, it is exactly what you wanted, comes with the pay and reward package you desire, you agree a start date and the deal is done. But this scenario doesn't always play out as straightforwardly as that – whether at the junior or senior level.

The promotion you are offered may not be the exact size and shape of the promotion you asked for. Perhaps it does not align with your intrinsic desire for a more meaningful role and the opportunity to really make a difference through your work. Maybe the company have offered you a promotion because a next-level-up role has become vacant, but it is not in an area of work that you are interested in, or the promotion requires a relocation. Perhaps it doesn't pay as well as you think it should in relation to the amount of extra responsibility you will have to shoulder.

Make sure you know what you are agreeing to in advance of saying yes. Usually the key decision-maker is the one who wants to tell you the good news that you have been promoted. They are typically very clear about the demands of the role, but often they are vague on the reward package details, and will pass you to HR to work through those. Ask for clear details on all aspects of what the promotion involves, and then find the compensating mechanisms that would make the deal more attractive for you. Be ready to negotiate your way forward to find a better solution for all parties.

Start by understanding exactly what is on offer:

- role title
- role responsibility
- pay and reward package
- role location
- start date
- future prospects

Then check in with yourself about whether this role will make you feel fulfilled and allow you to do meaningful work, and whether it will support your desire to make a difference and leave a positive leadership legacy behind. If you think this role promotion will make you seriously unhappy, then walk away from it, regardless of pay and reward – and think again about how to shift into a career path that will make you feel more connected and that has the right balance of extrinsic and intrinsic rewards.

Even assuming that this is the role promotion you wished for, unless the offer is a slam-dunk 'yes' on every aspect, I advise you to negotiate up. Your negotiating leverage in terms of pay and rewards will come from finding out what others are paid at this level. You may also want to think more creatively about what could be added into the reward package to sweeten the deal. If there is no budging on basic pay, could you negotiate a bonus-based income as an added extra, depending on what deals you bring in? Or could you be allowed to expense your travel pass, or to fly business class on trips, or are there any other ancillary benefits that you would value and enjoy?

If you aren't able to get the desired improvements in pay or rewards, can you be compensated in other ways? For example, could you negotiate a better title? You should always take the opportunity to try to make the title sound as senior as possible. Don't assume it has to be exactly the same title as the previous incumbent. A great title sends a clear message to your stake-holders and customers that you have secured an important position. Perhaps you could add 'Chief' or 'Senior'; or you could change the title by adding an 'and . . .', to better reflect any new extra responsibilities (e.g. Senior Managing Director and Head of Innovation). Maybe you could agree to modernize it entirely, to show the beneficial outcome of the role rather than the 'doing' part of the role, so from Head of Training to Head of Learning and Development, or from Head of Sales Support to Head of Customer Success. Your title is a great way to feel even more proud of yourself and what you do, and it should accurately reflect your personal role mission.

On the level of responsibility, if you want more then ask for more, and use this to negotiate up the pay and reward package – and then further negotiate on how to elevate the title!

All that being said, don't take too long to close the deal – because overly protracted negotiations may frustrate the decision-maker, who is now keen to have you on their team. They may question whether you are the right person for the role if you can't reach a conclusion within a reasonable time frame. At a certain point in the negotiations with HR and the decision-makers, be prepared to reach a balanced compromise. You won't usually get exactly what you want, so don't turn a negotiation into an argument. Sometimes the decision-maker may want to pay you more, but will be constrained by the norms of the organization. Be realistic and reasonable, and work together to agree on acceptable terms.

A promotion is essentially an opportunity to advance in your career, so think very carefully before you turn down a promotion. Consider how you might be able to take the offer and negotiate your way to a better outcome instead. Assess the opportunity in a big-picture, strategic way – and don't just think about what is right in front of you. Ask yourself these questions:

- Is the overall upside worth it? Does it bring you a step closer to your true dream role?

- Does it give you more responsibility, and more visibility with senior stakeholders – which could open up a wide network regarding promotion opportunities next time?

- Is it faster to take this promotion role and be better positioned next time for your ideal role, than it is to aim for one giant leap?

- What are the implications of saying 'no'? Would you be putting your future chances and even your employment in your current role at risk? Are you closing the door on ever being promoted in this company again?

If you are not at all happy with the promotion on offer and it is obvious that, no matter how much you try to negotiate for a better outcome, it is not the job you want – and if there will be no repercussions if you turn it down – then decline the promotion and wait for a better role to become available. But think about this very carefully, and ask yourself again: Will there really be no negative repercussions? How will stakeholders react?

You don't want to send out a signal that you are not ambitious and don't wish to progress further. You also don't want to get in the way of your future promotions.

Trust your instincts. If, on balance, the final negotiated promotion offer makes you feel excited, then go for it!

Frequently asked questions

Should I ever turn down a promotion?

Depending on the scarcity or otherwise of promotion opportunities at your company, then turning down a promotion could be quite risky. Is there a possibility of taking the promotion opportunity on offer and reshaping it or renegotiating it according to what you really want to do? If this is out of the question and there is no real upside in taking the promotion, and no real downside of not taking it, then communicate a clear case for why you don't want to accept the opportunity. Thank the decision-maker, and outline your alternative career ambitions. Enquire whether there is another promotion opportunity now or coming up soon which would work better both for the company and for you. The decision-maker will likely not be happy that you turned down the opportunity to work for them, so be sensitive to this and tread carefully – using all the diplomatic skills you can muster – to get them back onside. Ideally they will gain more of an understanding of what career path would suit you better, and they will see it as a win–win to support you in your ambitions and find a more suitable person for their role.

What if I receive a promotion but not a pay rise?

The worst-case scenario – and I have seen this happen – is when you are told you have a promotion, and you get a new title and extra responsibilities, but it doesn't come with any increase in pay! Just to be clear, a promotion without a pay rise is not actually a promotion. The promotion deal has to be a win for the company and a win for you.

A variation of this scenario is when you are offered a new role and told you will get a pay rise, but only after a year of proving yourself in the role. This also is not a promotion. Assert yourself – tell your future boss that you know you are worth more than this, and don't let anyone take advantage of you.

Should I quit if they refuse to promote me?

If your company refuses to promote you this time, ask for constructive feedback and consider whether you are likely to get the promotion next time. Take your cue from what they say. Obviously if they are very direct and say that you will never be promoted there, then you need to make plans to leave and join a company that will value you and open up future paths to promotion. If the situation is more ambiguous, it is up to you to work out what is really being said – and what you believe is true. Perhaps twelve months' more experience is exactly what you need to nail the promotion next time. However, as a general rule of thumb, if you have been declined for a promotion in two annual rounds – and your peers have started to move ahead of you – then I suggest that the company is sending you a signal that they are no longer committed to supporting your promotion success.

There is an unfortunate dynamic that occurs, which is that if you are passed over for promotion twice, then when your name comes up the next time, the decision-makers may decide not to risk promoting you just because you didn't get it the last two times! Although not logical, this does happen.

After two promotion rejections, then it is likely time to move on from the company. Just remember, it is always easier to get a new job if you have a job already, so don't quit straight away. Check if there are better promotion prospects in another part of the company. Then explore your options outside the organization, and weigh up whether it is better to stay or go – and when.

The good news is that when you follow the get-promoted game plan, you will feel much more in control of what promotion you want and why, and what steps you are taking to get there. You will feel more confident about your self-worth – and much better equipped to analyse why you have not been promoted so far, despite all your efforts. Don't take promotion rejection as a failure – instead see it as what it really is: just another experience in the rich tapestry of your working life. Learn from the experience, and then move on.

10 Congratulations, you got promoted!

Hit the ground running

Congratulations on securing your promotion!

Now build on the momentum of your promotion success: hit the ground running in the first 100 days of your new role, and set yourself up to get promoted faster next time. All eyes will be on you in those first 100 days, so you need to be impressive from the outset. Take the central message of empowerment from this book, and apply it in your new role to ensure further success. Revisit your First 100 Days document that you created as part of your get-promoted campaign. Discuss expectations with role stakeholders, confirm your three-year vision, your first-year priorities, and refresh your plan accordingly. Update and improve it based on any new role context.

The importance of the first 100 days in your new role

Judgements of a leader's success in the first 100 days of a new role can be followed quickly by judgements about their leadership potential for success in the next-step-up role in two to three years' time. It is as simple as this – if you care enough to invest in doing a great job in your first 100 days, you will be noticed by your boss and others, and promotion naturally follows. The opposite is also true. If you get off to a slow start, then imagine how much more difficult it will be to claw back lost time in an attempt to succeed later. If you fail to get it right from the beginning, then you seriously risk your chances of success in this role, which can stall or reduce your future career prospects.[1]

Get role-ready before your official start date. In particular, pay attention to the following:

- *Letting go of your current role responsibilities*
  Your current role is coming to a close, so start to hand it over to your successor as quickly as possible. Don't be overly attached to projects that are under way and not yet complete. Do what you can before you leave, but shift the majority of your focus and attention onto the new role.

- *Anticipating role transition challenges*
  Consider the likely transition challenges and where the pitfalls of the new role may lie. What could you do now, in anticipation, so that you are able to make a strong start in your new role? How do you flatten the learning curve, who could give you advice, should you invest in an executive coach for your first 100 days?

---

1 Extract from my book *Your First 100 Days: How to make maximum impact in your new leadership role.*

- *Profiling your team – capability and gaps*
  Find out who will be on your team, and consider their
  capability to deliver on your vision and plans. Where might
  the gaps be? Think about what recruitment searches you
  may need to launch on arrival in your new role. Building a
  high-performing team will be critical in the first 100 days –
  and will play a major determining role in future successes
  and promotions.

Get promoted faster next time

Now that you have unlocked the mystery of how to get this
promotion, I am confident you will get promoted even faster
next time. I have worked with clients on consecutive promotions, each one faster and easier than the last.

Don't wait two or three years before you start to think about
your next promotion. Plan it from day one. Ensure maximum
impact in your new role, incorporating all the insights and advice from this book into your day-to-day approach. Pick up
this book from time to time as a refresher, to ensure you are
covering all the right get-promoted moves to get you to the
next level up.

Success will be when you don't need this book any more, and
you feel fully empowered to shape a better future for yourself.
Continue to push yourself forward, to learn, to grow, to
develop – and to become the great leader I know you can be.

Good luck on your journey, and thank you for reading this
book.

Index

Page references in *italics* indicate images.

PENGUIN PARTNERSHIPS

Penguin Partnerships is the Creative Sales and Promotions team at Penguin Random House. We have a long history of working with clients on a wide variety of briefs, specializing in brand promotions, bespoke publishing and retail exclusives, plus corporate, entertainment and media partnerships.

We can respond quickly to briefs and specialize in repurposing books and content for sales promotions, for use as incentives and retail exclusives as well as creating content for new books in collaboration with our partners as part of branded book relationships.

Equally if you'd simply like to buy a bulk quantity of one of our existing books at a special discount, we can help with that too. Our books can make excellent corporate or employee gifts.

Special editions, including personalized covers, excerpts of existing books or books with corporate logos can be created in large quantities for special needs.

We can work within your budget to deliver whatever you want, however you want it.

For more information, please contact
salesenquiries@penguinrandomhouse.co.uk